ORIGIN

What Really Happened In The Beginning

Nycole Donelson

DIANGELLO

PUBLISHING

MOST DIANGELLO PUBLISHING products are available at special quantity discounts for bulk purchases for sales promotions, fundraising and educational needs. For details, email create@diangellopublishing.com.

ORIGIN: WHAT REALLY HAPPENED IN THE BEGINNING by Nycole Donelson

Published by Diangello Publishing
40 Burton Hills Blvd
Suite 200
Nashville, TN 37215
www.DiangelloPublishing.com

Unless otherwise noted, all Scripture quotations are taken from the King James Version of the Holy Bible.

Cover design by Elev8art • www.elev8art.net

Author's Photograph by Roberto "Tito" Machado Sitzler

Visit the author's website at www.nycoledonelson.com

Library of Congress Cataloging-in-Publication Data:
2022902755

ISBN: 979-8-9858700-4-6

ISBN: 979-8-9858700-0-8 (E-book)

Capitalization

Nycole has taken *Author's Prerogative* in capitalizing certain words which are not usually capitalized according to standard grammatical practice. This has been done for the purpose of highlighting the Deity of God.

CONTENTS

Introduction..vii

Day 1..1
    Heaven And Earth...............................3
    Darkness And Deep.............................5
    The Spirit Of God..............................9
    Light..11

Day 2..15
    Firmament......................................17

Day 3..19
    Earth Realm And Production...............21

Day 4..25
    Lights...27
    Evening And Morning........................36

Day 5 - 5th Setting of Order.......................49
    Water Creature And Fowl...................51
    Fowl That May Fly Above The Earth......52
    Moving Creature...............................54
    Life From The Waters.........................59

Day 6 - 6th Setting Of Order......................63
    Land Animals And Man......................65
    Beast, Cattle And Creeping Things........67

Man...69

Image...72

Likeness..78

Formed...84

The Breath, The Nostrils And
The Soul..88

The Breath...89

The Nostrils.......................................90

The Soul..92

The Move Of God.................................99

Differences Between Genesis 1
And Genesis 2...................................104

Placement..110

Who Was Present?...............................117

The Trinity..123

The Father...124

Day 7 - 7th Setting of Order....................131

Rest...133

The Blueprint......................................137

Notes..143

INTRODUCTION

T his book discusses a topic that I believe everyone has heard about, either in a religious setting or in an educational setting, but perhaps not quite like this.

I am going to be discussing scripture found in the Book of Genesis. The Book of Genesis plays a very important role in Christianity as it details the beginning of the world as well as the history of the Israelite nation which began with our covenant fathers Abraham, Isaac and Jacob. A nation that initiated and ultimately solidified our relationship with God through Jesus the Christ.

The word *Genesis* is defined as "origin" in the Hebrew language and it is translated as "in the beginning".[1] Therefore, the Book of Genesis has been adequately named as it details the origin, the beginning of everything, except God Himself.

The Book of Genesis is the origin of...

The Word of God
The world
Humankind
Sin in the world
God's promise of redemption
Humankind's relationship with God
God revealing Himself and His immeasurable love
...and that is where we are going to aim this discussion - with the Book of Genesis beginning to reveal God to us.

In a nutshell, we find the Book of Genesis reveals humankind's:

- Creation/Origination
- Deterioration
- Restoration

With this information in mind, I have entitled this book: Origin - What really happened in the beginning.

As you prepare to read this book, it is my intention to reveal several things about The Creation - primarily the origin of the world and humankind. After reading this book, you should come to understand what happened in the beginning including: God's intention for bringing forth light, the composition and true purpose of man, as well as decipher how The Trinity was involved in The Creation.

Before we begin, there are a few tips to get the most understanding out of this book:

1. *Pay close attention* - I will be presenting a perspective that will challenge what you may believe occurred during The

Creation. It will reveal what God really had in mind when He began His creative endeavor and, most importantly, it will reveal what God designed for you.

2. *Forget What You Think You Know!* - The information discussed in this book will challenge your perception and intellectual understanding of how the world was formed. The Bible is not a natural book - it is a spiritual text. Therefore, a natural mind needs to learn through a deeper understanding which is revealed by the Spirit of God.

Throughout this book, we will discuss the entire chapter of Genesis 1 and the majority of Genesis 2. I am going to review the scripture in stages. As I dissect the aforementioned chapters, unless otherwise stated, I will be utilizing Biblical Hebrew definitions to expound on keywords and phrases. This is necessary because the original language of the Old Testament was written in Hebrew and defining the words according to the original language will bring clarity to the scripture.

Are you ready?

Let's go!

DAY 1

In the beginning God created the heaven and the earth.

And the earth was without form, and void; and darkness was upon the face of the deep. And the Spirit of God moved upon the face of the waters.

And God said, Let there be light: and there was light.

And God saw the light, that it was good: and God divided the light from the darkness.

And God called the light Day, and the darkness he called Night. And the evening and the morning were the first day.

Genesis 1:1-5

1

HEAVEN AND EARTH

*In the beginning God created the heaven
and the earth.*

*And the earth was without form, and void;
and darkness was upon the face of the deep.
And the Spirit of God moved upon the face
of the waters.*

Genesis 1:1-2

The Bible begins by stating that God created the heaven and the earth. You may be thinking that *heaven* is the sky which can be physically seen from earth. In this context, *heaven* is defined as "the invisible realm of God"[2] which tells us the heaven God created in the beginning is the heavenly (spiritual) realm. Alternatively, the word *earth* is defined as "world or earth",[3] which refers to the earthly (natural) realm. According to Genesis 1:2, God created the heaven and the earth, but only the earth "was without form and void". The earthly realm was formless, empty, desolate and useless and although it had been created, the world was not visible because it had not been formed. With this context, Genesis 1:1 reads as:

> *In the beginning, God created the heavenly*
> *(spiritual) realm and the earthly (natural)*
> *realm.*

DARKNESS AND DEEP

As noted in the previous chapter, Genesis 1:2 also tells us that darkness was upon the face of the deep.

The word *darkness* is defined as "dark, blackness, often with the associative meaning of gloom, despair, terror, ignorance or hard to understand".[4] In the English language, *darkness* is defined as "the total absence of light"[5].

The word *deep* refers to "the depths, with associative meanings of darkness and secrecy, controlled or inhabited by mysterious powers; the depths of the earth is the abode of the dead".[6]

Now that we understand the meaning of *darkness* and *deep* in relation to Genesis 1:2, then we must consider that if the deep is associated with darkness, then the gloom, despair, terror, ignorance, the hard to understand, and the total absence of light, alluding to a secret mysterious power that controls or inhabits the abode or place of the dead, was present in the beginning.

Over the next several chapters, I will repeatedly express the meaning of darkness because I want to clarify what darkness truly is. People often associate negative feelings or characteristics as human; however, these feelings have an influence which is a secret mysterious power that controls the abode of the dead. Darkness is a being with a purpose - a *who*, not an *it*. I hope to illuminate these notions in the remainder of this book with the hope of uncovering who is

5

governing the tumultuous feelings in our lives.

Do you have an idea of who darkness is? Darkness is not a normal occurrence to humankind. Darkness is an influence. An influence of gloom, despair, terror, ignorance, the hard to understand, the total absence of light, and motivated by a secret, mysterious power that controls or inhabits the abode of the dead. The Apostle Paul helps us to understand who darkness is by stating:

> *"For we wrestle not against flesh and blood, but against principalities, against powers, against the rulers of the darkness of this world, against spiritual wickedness in high places." - Ephesians 6:12*

This darkness - which is the influence of gloom, despair, terror, ignorance, the hard to understand, and the total absence of light that controls or inhabits the abode of the dead - that was present in the beginning, is our enemy, the devil, Satan and his cohorts. The devil's goal is threefold: to attack you physically, mentally and spiritually. We see this concept clearly in the account of the plagues upon Egypt when Pharaoh refused to release the children of Israel in Exodus 10:21-23.

> *And the Lord said unto Moses, Stretch out thine hand toward heaven, that there may be darkness over the land of Egypt, even darkness which may be felt.*
>
> *And Moses stretched forth his hand toward heaven; and there was a thick darkness in*

all the land of Egypt three days:

They saw not one another, neither rose any
from his place for three days: but all the chil-
dren of Israel had light in their dwellings.

Exodus 10:21–23

The Biblical account of the nine Egyptian plagues indicate that the last plague of darkness that came over the land of Egypt was so thick that it could be felt. It kept people from seeing or looking at anyone else, and even prevented people from getting up for three days. Gloom, despair, and terror immobilized everyone that was in darkness.

Can you see the influence of darkness? It affects you mentally with feelings of gloom, despair and terror, designed to keep you in a crippled state, unable or unwilling to function or physically move about in your daily tasks. This is a one-two punch (physical and mental) that the enemy uses to attack you. Ironically, after Pharoah experienced the thick darkness for three days, he decided to let the children of Israel go as requested. This physical and mental affliction was clearly evident upon the Egyptians.

The third method of the enemy's tactic uses darkness to target you spiritually with the hopes of making you spiritually blind and having no understanding and no light into the things of God. 2 Corinthians 4:4 tells us that:

> *"...the god of this world hath blinded the*
> *minds of the lost, those which believe not,*
> *lest the light of the glorious gospel of Christ,*
> *who is the image of God, should shine unto*

them."

All three methods of the enemy are deployed against you to bring you out of your relationship and dependency on God and draw you into a vulnerable place where the devil can have access to your soul.

THE SPIRIT OF GOD

Let's continue with the latter part of Genesis 1:2 which tells us that "the Spirit of God moved upon the face of the waters".

Did you notice that the Spirit of God is the only One noted as having movement in this verse? The meaning of the word *moved* is "to tremble or shake".[7]

That tells us that the Spirit of God was able to move the waters and both existed and operated in the midst of darkness. Despite Satan controlling and inhabiting the abode of the dead, the Spirit of God was present and still functioned.

Remember, the Spirit of God was upon the face of the waters so, wherever there were waters, there was the Spirit of God's ability to move. What I am trying to get you to perceive is that darkness - the gloom, despair, terror, ignorance, the hard to understand, the total absence of light, the secret mysterious power that controls or inhabits the abode of the dead, also known as Satan, does not have power over the Spirit of God. Satan, nor his influence, did not have power over the Spirit of God then and he nor his devices have power over the Spirit of God now!

That's great news, but there is more!

Let's look at Genesis 1:2 a little closer. Verse 2 says that "the Spirit of God moved upon the face of the waters".

Until now, according to Genesis 1:1-2, the Bible only

mentioned heaven, the world, darkness and the deep. If the Spirit of God moved upon the face of the waters (not water, but waters - *plural*), what does that mean?

Let's jump ahead a few scriptures and check out Genesis 1:6 which reads:

> And God said, Let there be a firmament in
> the midst of the waters, and let it divide the
> waters from the waters.

The Spirit of God moved upon the face of the waters which were everywhere and the Spirit of God had all power over them. That tells us that in the beginning there were all waters in the spiritual and earthly realms, as well as the Spirit of God, darkness and the deep, but no world because, at this time, the world had not been formed yet. If you are wondering how there could be waters without the world, remember that the world was formless, empty, desolate, useless without producing anything. That means, there was nothing.

Interesting, but before we get too far off course, let's continue with reading about The Creation in succession. We have begun understanding what occurred on day 1 of The Creation by dissecting Genesis 1:1-2, now let's continue with what occurred on the remainder of day 1 by examining Genesis 1:3-5.

LIGHT

And God said, Let there be light: and there was light.

And God saw the light, that it was good: and God divided the light from the darkness.

And God called the light Day, and the darkness he called Night. And the evening and the morning were the first day.

Genesis 1:3-5

Did you notice the Bible did not state that God created light? Scripture indicated that God said, "Let there be light." You see, darkness was already present and it was upon the face of the deep. God didn't need to create darkness as it was already in existence. Instead, God brought forth light and He did so by simply speaking. In the previous chapter, we discussed that, in the beginning, *waters* were everywhere. Therefore, when God brought forth light, the light was in the midst of the waters.

Considering the first three verses of Genesis chapter 1, we have the spiritual and earthly realms, the darkness and deep, the Spirit of God, the waters and the light all present in the beginning. Now that we understand the activity of day 1, we understand that the first thing God brought forth in the beginning was light into the spiritual and earthly realms. God provided light by speaking. Incidentally, there

11

is no mention of the spiritual or earthly realms being spoken into existence. The Bible indicates that God created them. Why did God "bring forth" light, but "create" the spiritual and earthly realms?

> God didn't have to "create" light because
> He already had light. Light was part of Him.
> He just gave light.

Scripture then says that after God gave light, He separated light from darkness. God separated the light from the gloom, despair, terror, ignorance, the hard to understand, the total absence of light, that secret, mysterious power which controls or inhabits the abode of the dead. God separated light from the influences of Satan and this culminated the first day, which was evening and morning.

Let's review what we have come to learn thus far.

Day 1 - God brought forth light. We see separation, a distinction **of** light **from** darkness (from gloom, despair, terror, ignorance, the hard to understand, the total absence of light, the secret mysterious power that controls and inhabits the abode of the dead; Satan) and evening, morning and day were called. God also puts light in the midst of the waters which are everywhere in the spiritual and earthly realms. We discovered that light is not separate or distinct from the Spirit of God moving on the waters, but it is separate and distinct from darkness which is Satan. The light being brought forth did not affect the waters and it did not affect the Spirit of God's movement. The purpose of the light, according to verse 4, was to be divided from darkness, from Satan, from the gloom, despair, terror, ignorance, the hard to understand, and the total absence of light that is the secret mysterious power that controls and inhabits the abode of the dead in the spiritual and the earthly realms... and God saw that it was good.

DAY 2

And God said, Let there be a firmament in the midst of the waters, and let it divide the waters from the waters.

And God made the firmament, and divided the waters which were under the firmament from the waters which were above the firmament: and it was so.

And God called the firmament Heaven. And the evening and the morning were the second day.

Genesis 1:6-8

FIRMAMENT

W e learned in Genesis 1:2, that the Spirit of God is moving upon all the waters, which meant that in the beginning, the Spirit of God was everywhere.

Proceeding to Genesis 1:6, we are informed that God made a firmament in the midst of the waters which He names *Heaven*. The word *firmament* is defined as "the expanse, or a continuous space".[8] This refers to what we call "the sky".

This firmament called *Heaven* is not the same heaven as stated in Genesis 1:1. Remember, that was referred to as the spiritual realm. Here, in verse 8, Heaven is "the expanse or continuous space". What we see is that on day 2, God made a continuous space in the midst of the waters, which splits them. He rearranged the waters that were already in the spiritual and earthly realms upon which His Spirit is moving and He divided the waters horizontally in two, but the darkness nor the deep were displaced. And the evening and the morning were the second day.

I have always been taught, and also taught others that the firmament called *Heaven* and the world we call *Earth* were created on the same day. When writing this book, Holy Spirit caused me to see that teaching as inaccurate. If you pay close attention to Genesis 1:8, you will discover that the only activity God performed on day 2 was to create the expanse in the midst of the waters and name the open space "Heaven". The creation of Earth is discussed later in Genesis 1:9-10, which informs us of the activities of day 3. Let's go there now.

DAY 3

And God said, Let the waters under the heaven be gathered together unto one place, and let the dry land appear: and it was so.

And God called the dry land Earth; and the gathering together of the waters called he Seas: and God saw that it was good.

And God said, Let the earth bring forth grass, the herb yielding seed, and the fruit tree yielding fruit after his kind, whose seed is in itself, upon the earth: and it was so.

And the earth brought forth grass, and herb yielding seed after his kind, and the tree yielding fruit, whose seed was in itself, after his kind: and God saw that it was good.

And the evening and the morning were the third day.

Genesis 1:9-13

EARTH REALM AND PRODUCTION

In the previous chapter, we learned that God dissected the waters that the Spirit of God moved upon by creating an "expanse or continuous space" in the midst of the waters. It is now day 3 and scripture reveals that God commands the waters that are under the expanse to gather in one place. In this context, the word *gather* means "to wait".[9] Essentially, God told the waters below the expanse to, "stay where I set you or delay action until I instruct you to move". By the command of God, the waters move to a certain place and dry ground appears. At this time, the separation of waters from dry ground takes place. The dry ground God calls *Earth* and the waters God commanded to "stay put until further notice", He calls *Seas* and God saw that it was good.

God then speaks to Earth, which is dry ground, and tells the Earth to bring forth. The term *bring forth* means "to become green of pastures and produce".[10] What exactly did God tell the dry ground to bring forth? Genesis 1:11-12 in-

21

dicates that God told the dry ground to make green of pasture and produce grass, the herb yielding seed, and the fruit tree yielding fruit after his kind, whose seed is in itself. How do these categories of produce differ from each other? Let's look at a few definitions.

The word *grass* is defined as "(new) green vegetation, (new) green grass or tender grass".[11]

The word *herb* is defined as "green plant, vegetation, grass, herb". [12]

Yielding means "to sow seed, to plant seed, to become pregnant".[13]

Seed is defined as "seed, semen, that which propagates a species".[14]

Fruit means "produce, by extension: offspring of any creature; result of any action".[15]

The word *kind* here means "genus or species".[16]

Taking a closer look at the meaning of these words, we see that grass and herb allude to vegetation, which sows seed. Seed in vegetation has a cycle of growth generated from it's natural spreading, therefore the seed from vegetation has the ability to release and sow its own seed and initiate the production of more vegetation. If you are having trouble grasping this concept, think of weeds. I have never, ever, planted seed for a weed; however, they continually show up uninvited in my lawn most of the year. This occurs because the weed has a seed and when it's seed is blown and lands on dry ground, that seed takes root and grows.

Grass and herb are different from the fruit tree yielding fruit whose seed is in itself. Based on the above definition, we also discovered that unlike the grass and herb, the tree becomes pregnant and bears the fruit. However, it is the fruit that carries the seed that will need to be cultivated in order to produce more fruit trees. This helps us to understand why God said that the fruit tree yields fruit whose seed is in itself as opposed to the grass and herb which yield seed.

Lastly, Genesis 1:12 states that grass and herb yielding seed would be after his kind and the fruit tree was to yield fruit after his kind. As expressed above, the word "kind" refers to a genus, species or to say it plainly its a group with similar features. God makes it plain that whether the ground produces rye, lemongrass, wheat, or corn - they are all of the vegetative species, despite the fact that they are all different types of vegetation. It is the same with the fruit tree. Regardless, if a variety of trees produce figs, lemon, avocado or peaches, then they are all fruit trees - just different types of the fruit species. Therefore, what the grass and herb, as well as the fruit tree produced was not indicative of one type of vegetation or a single type of fruit, but a variation of each, and yet the variation did not change how they were originally created or to which group or "kind" they belonged.

Something very fascinating happened on day 3. If you were paying attention, you learned of the *forming of the world*. Recall, in Genesis 1:2, the earthly realm was *without form and void* - which translates to the world being empty, a waste, and desolate. Alternatively, the word *form* means "to appear or manifest".[17] Once God shifted the waters and dry ground appeared, the world was now formed. How do I know? This dry ground called Earth is not the same *earth* as stated in Genesis 1:1. Remember, the earth in Genesis 1:1 is the earthly (natural) realm. Here, in verse 10, Earth is the manifested world as God called the dry ground Earth! Therefore, the earthly realm is no longer without form and void because God has now configured and caused dry ground and vegetation to appear along with the Seas.

Ultimately, God speaks to the waters in the earthly (natural) realm causing them to gather which resulted in the appearance of the dry ground. He then commands the dry ground to produce two types of food: vegetation and fruit. This earthly realm, which was once a place that was desolate, empty, useless and not producing, without form and void, He now instructs to produce. The earthly realm was obedient and God saw that it was good.

DAY 4

And God said, Let there be lights in the firmament of the heaven to divide the day from the night; and let them be for signs, and for seasons, and for days, and years:

And let them be for lights in the firmament of the heaven to give light upon the earth: and it was so.

And God made two great lights; the greater light to rule the day, and the lesser light to rule the night: he made the stars also.

And God set them in the firmament of the heaven to give light upon the earth,

And to rule over the day and over the night, and to divide the light from the darkness: and God saw that it was good.

25

*And the evening and the morning were the
fourth day.*

Genesis 1:14-19

LIGHTS

Day 4 begins with God bringing lights into the expanse or the continuous space that He had set in place on day 2.

In this context, the word *lights* is defined as "light source, luminary, light-bearer".[18]

God made lights: the greater (larger) light which is the sun, the lesser (smaller) light being the moon, and the stars, some of which are planets. Ironically, science refers to the sun as a star and it is the closest star to Earth.

According to verses 14-18, God's purpose for lights was "to be for lights in the expanse of the firmament, to provide light upon the earth and to rule over the day and over the night and to divide the light from the darkness on the earth, and to be for signs, seasons, days and years".

27

Up to this point, there was light, the Spirit of God everywhere, waters, darkness (gloom, terror, despair, ignorance, the hard to understand, the total absence of light which is the secret mysterious power that controls and inhabits the abode of the dead), heaven (spiritual realm), firmament/ Heaven (expanse) and Earth (dry ground - earthly realm), day and night, evening, morning, vegetation and now God adds lights (sun, moon, planets, and stars).

Remember, I showed you that **light** was brought forth on day 1, before Heaven was created on day 2. Earth appeared and vegetation came forth on day 3 prior to **the lights** (sun, moon, planets, and stars) which were made and placed in the firmament on day 4.

Do you see anything interesting?

A question to consider.

If the sun was made on day 4, how can it be that no sun was required for light as a visual brightness or as a light source during the day, morning or evening of days 1, 2 and 3?

I am going to address this question in detail, but let's start with this:

The lights (sun, moon, planets, and stars) were made *after* the vegetation. I find that interesting because my husband and I garden and all the instructions that are provided with the seeds or seedlings tell us that they require at least 6-8 hours of direct sunlight to produce a harvest. How is it that the sun that God created on day 4 was not required for light for the vegetation that He commanded to grow the day before?

Now, I can imagine that many of you have come up with a response.

- The vegetation was just created the day before, therefore no light was necessary or..

- The light that God brought forth on day 1 provided light for the vegetation.

In the Introduction of this book, I asked you to forget what you think you know. This is why. No matter your thought process, the implication here is that the vegetation didn't need the lights (sun) to grow or for nourishment.

Vegetation didn't need lights (sun) to grow because God had already grown the vegetation and He is able to maintain the vegetation without the sun. God created and sustained them. God is Omnipotent, all powerful and does not need what man thinks or what man says. He can do anything, which tells us the lights created on day 4, the sun, moon, planets, and stars were created for a different purpose than the light He brought forth on day 1. In other words, there was a reason God brought forth the light before He made the lights.

By day 4, light was already present and it was separate and divided from the darkness. The purpose of the light on day 1, according to verse 4, was to *be divided from darkness*, divided from the gloom, despair, terror, ignorance, the hard to understand and total absence of light, that secret mysterious power that controls the abode of the dead. Which means light and darkness coexisted. They were in the same place at the same time, but God made them not to intermingle, they had nothing of the other in them. God separated light and darkness and made a clear distinction between light and darkness. However, God's purpose for the lights on day 4 (the sun, moon, planets, and stars) was to *provide light upon the earth and to rule over the day and over the night, to divide the light from the darkness on the earth; and to be for signs, seasons, days and years.*

Let's look at this a bit closer. There are several things going on here.

If God had already divided the light from the darkness on day 1, which light He called *Day* and darkness He called *Night*, why divide day and night with lights on day 4?

Let's go back and take a closer look at Genesis 1:1-5.

> *In the beginning God created the heaven and the earth.*
>
> *And the earth was without form, and void; and darkness was upon the face of the deep. And the Spirit of God moved upon the face of the waters.*
>
> *And God said, Let there be light: and there was light.*
>
> *And God saw the light, that it was good: and God divided the light from the darkness.*
>
> *And God called the light Day, and the darkness he called Night. And the evening and*

the morning were the first day.

Now, I would like you to focus on verse 5.

Day 1: The Light is called *Day*, the Darkness is called *Night*, and evening and morning are the 1st day.

Let's spend a little time discussing the word "day".

If I were to refer to "today", when did this day begin? You would likely respond "12:00 AM or midnight".

If I ask, "When will this day end?" You would likely respond, "11:59 PM".

If I were to say "come by the next day." When does the next day begin? You would likely respond "12:00 AM or midnight".

If you have answered the questions as expected, all of your responses refer to "a day" as 12:00 AM - 11:59 PM, which is a continual cycle. Hence, *Day* in this context is independent of light or dark hours. What I want to convey is that light called *Day* in day 1 was not referring to daylight.

> Light in day 1 is not a reference to time; it is referring to continuity, a consistent action that does not stop.

As we look at the definition within the original language of Biblical words, as with most languages, you will find that words often have more than one meaning and usage of their meanings must be used in context to the text you are studying. With this in mind, consider the meaning of the words "day" and "night" and you will see multiple definitions. The appropriate meaning in context to our scripture is highlighted below.

The word *day* is defined as "day (**24 hours**); daytime (in contrast to night)".[19]

If day is in contrast to night, let's look at the meaning of night.

The word *night* "bears the implication of **continuous illicit, illegal or immoral activity**".[20]

What exactly is illicit, immoral and illegal activity? Let's check it out.

The word *illicit* is defined as "forbidden by law, rules, or custom".[21]

Illegal is defined as "contrary to or forbidden by law, especially criminal law".[22]

Immoral is defined as "not conforming to accepted standards of morality".[23]

Now, let's recollect the succession of creation. On day 1, what was present in the spiritual and earthly realms? Light, which God called Day, and darkness which God called Night. The Spirit of God as well as the deep and waters were also present.

Did you notice that on day 1 nothing had been created yet? That means there was no man created on the earth on day 1. Now, hold on to your thoughts here as we move forward in defining night.

If you consider the above definition of night, then this

illicit, illegal, immoral activity was not relating to the behavior of man. How is that possible? If you think back to the previous chapter, everything was taking place in the spiritual and earthly realms because nothing had been created - surely not man.

> This illegal, illicit, immoral activity was
> spiritual and not referring to man's behavior
> or way of living.

The word *night* in this context refers to illegal, illicit, immoral activity according to God's way of doing things - which is His righteousness. Therefore, God is revealing to us that gloom, despair, terror, ignorance, the hard to understand, the total absence of light which is a secret mysterious power that controls the abode of the dead *is* illicit, immoral and illegal activity in the spiritual and in the earthly realms!

Genesis 1:4 confirms this concept in the following verse:

> *And God saw the light, that it was good: and*
> *God divided the light from the darkness.*

God said only the light was good. The word *good* is defined as "pleasing, desirable, which refers to **quality as well as moral goodness**".[24]

If darkness is also night which is spiritually improper activity, and you understand that the word *day* is a continual process of 24 hours, then light called Day is referring to continuous moral goodness and darkness is referring to continual illicit, immoral, illegal activity.

What God did on day 1 was to separate the spiritually good (light which He called Day) from the spiritually illicit, immoral, illegal activity (darkness which He called Night). Darkness was already present when light was brought forth and, because God determined darkness was not moral goodness, He brought forth light.

Do you see that?

God called the light "Day" and light was present before the world was created. Light was also present before time was created, therefore, light called *Day* was to exist always - among, yet separate, from the darkness called *Night* which was also present before time and before the world was created.

This tells us that the light (Day) and the darkness (Night) that was present on day 1 wasn't about instituting time for men nor were they in the firmament that God created on day 2. Both light and darkness existed prior to the world being created. They both existed in the spiritual and earthly realms along with the Spirit of God. What God did by bringing forth light in the presence of darkness was done in the spiritual and earthly realms.

Thus, what light is really referring to on day 1 is not a light as in brightness or a light source, but as something of moral goodness, separate and distinct from spiritually illicit, immoral and illegal activity. This light, called Day, stays around continually and is distinct from the darkness called Night.

Let's keep talking because, as of yet, there is no reference of time mentioned. We have discovered that Day and Night as well as light and darkness are not referencing the institution of time for humankind, more so they refer to spiritual activity.

EVENING AND MORNING

Although Day remains forever and is continual, never ending, and not conformed to time, it keeps going. Now, we see evening and morning introduced when God says that "evening and morning are the first day."

Now wait a minute! We just learned that the words *Day* and *Night* previously stated in this passage was not a declaration of time, but *Day* and *Night* referred to moral versus immoral activity. If *Day* and *Night* are not a reference of time, how are evening and morning the first *day*? I would like to show you how evening and morning have different meanings in this context in the same way that day and night had a different meaning!

The world often uses the term evening and night interchangeably. Similarly, the world considers day and morning the same, both determined by the rising and setting of the sun. However, scripturally, there is a difference.

When did God first refer to evening and morning? Day 1

When was the world created? Day 2

We see that the Bible indicated the inception of evening and morning **before** the world appeared and time was created.

We have already ascertained that on day 1, when God called light *"Day"*, that this was not a declaration of time but a continual separation of moral activity from immoral activity. If *Day* and *Night* were not about time, then evening and morning are not about time either. What does evening and morning refer to then?

In order to answer that question I conducted a Hebrew word study and I have deduced that the word *evening* comes from the base meaning of chaos, an increasing state of disorder, and obscurity.

The word *morning* is the opposite of evening. Morning is when light breaks the darkness. Therefore, morning is when chaos or the state of disorder decreases and order occurs.

Let's dig a little deeper.

I think it would be helpful to define a few more words that were noted in the above definitions.

The word *chaos* is defined as "complete disorder and confusion".[25]

Disorder means "to disrupt the systematic functioning".[26]

Order means "to give an authoritative direction or instruction to do something; the arrangement or disposition of people or things in relation to each other according to a particular sequence, pattern or method".[27]

We see the definition of *chaos* as confusion, but 1 Corinthians 14:33 states:

> *For God is not the author of confusion, but of*
> *peace, as in all churches of the saints.*

Therefore, chaos nor confusion comes from God. Additionally, looking closely at the definition of *order*, there is one more word that caught my attention and I think it would also be helpful to define.

As stated above, *order* means "to give an authoritative direction or instruction to do something; the arrangement or disposition of people or things in relation to each other according to a particular sequence, *pattern*, or method".[27]

The word *pattern* stands out to me and it is defined as "a regularity in the world".[28]

Based on the understanding of the words *evening and morning*, where evening means chaos and disorder; and morning means the decreasing of chaos and disorder, we understand then that evening and morning are referring to the transition between the two:

Going From Chaos to Order!

We know that God is a God of order.

Remember that the word '*Day*' in this context is referring to continual progress and not referring to time. So when the Bible stated that evening and morning were the first day, it was indicating the first continual thing that God brought from chaos to order was presenting good and making it distinct from darkness. Instituting morality in the midst of illicit, immoral and illegal activity continually.

Let's look at this a little closer.

God took what was in disorder and brought order. But, what was in disorder in the beginning? The disorder was darkness - the gloom, terror, dread, ignorance, the hard to understand, the total absence of light which is the secret mysterious power that controls and inhabits the abode of the dead, which is illicit, immoral and illegal activity.

When God brought forth light, He was bringing order into a place of chaos! He was causing moral goodness to be present and to be separate and distinct from immoral activity.

If you haven't figured it out by now, I am going to tell you what The Creation is really about. I'm going to tell you what really happened in the beginning.

The Creation is more than just making a heaven and an earth. Tossing in vegetation, animals and a few people. The Creation reveals that God is setting up how He wants things to be for this world as well as in the spiritual and earthly realms. It is about God setting *order* and setting His *pattern* which was defined a moment ago as regularity in the world.

Therefore, in the beginning, the setting of order is God's way of doing things. The Creation is about setting order and the first thing God does is provide a distinction between good in His righteousness and immoral spiritual influences in the spiritual and earthly realms. By adding light, God is ultimately showing His glory by bringing forth light among the darkness.

> Days 1 through 3 are not about time -
> they are about <u>order</u> !

So, in the beginning, we see God in the spiritual realm setting order for the earthly realm prior to the world being

39

formed!

With that in mind - let's review what God really did on days 1 through 3.

From now on, when the Bible indicates that "evening and morning were the # day", I am going to replace the "# day" with the "# of setting of order" as shown below:

Day 1 - 1st setting of order:
Establishing what is good (moral activity) based on what God determines. Setting the pattern of good/moral versus immoral.

Day 2 - 2nd setting of order:
Setting the pattern of the earthly realm in the midst of the spiritual realm.

Day 3 - 3rd setting of order:
Setting the pattern of reproduction for the earthly realm.

Let's return to where we left off before being sidetracked. I was discussing lights on day 4, or the 4th setting of order.

It has now been revealed that light in the 1st setting of order (previously referred to as day 1) is truly different from the lights noted in the 4th setting of order (previously referred to as day 4).

Day 4 - 4th Setting of Order

And God said, Let there be lights in the firmament of the heaven to divide the day from the night; and let them be for signs, and for seasons, and for days, and years:

And let them be for lights in the firmament of the heaven to give light upon the earth: and it was so.

And God made two great lights; the greater light to rule the day, and the lesser light to rule the night: he made the stars also.

And God set them in the firmament of the heaven to give light upon the earth,

And to rule over the day and over the night, and to divide the light from the darkness: and God saw that it was good.

And the evening and the morning were the fourth day.

Genesis 1:14-19

As you can see, scripture indicates two purposes for the creation of lights.

According to verse 16, the first purpose of lights - the sun and the moon - is to rule in the firmament of the heaven and provide a light source **upon** the earth.

The second purpose of lights, as shown in verse 14 is for signs, for seasons, for days and years.

The first purpose of lights is evident; however, I would like to further examine God's intention for the second purpose of these lights. As stated previously, definitions of the

41

original Hebrew language of Biblical words often have more than one meaning, usage of the meanings must be used in context to the text that you are studying. Based on this understanding, if one word has multiple definitions, the highlighted words below coincide with our context.

The word *signs* is defined as "a mark, symbol, **a signal or event that communicates**, a supernatural event or miracle as a sign from God".[29]

If you have ever traveled anywhere by automobile, you can determine how close you are to your destination based on the signs.

The word *seasons* is defined as "**Tent of Meeting, appointed time, designated time**, season, **set feasts and sacred days**". [30]

As I have previously noted, the word *days* is defined as "a day (24 hours); **daytime** (in contrast to night)".[19] In this context, day is referring to *time*.

The word *years* is defined as "the time taken by the earth to make one revolution around the sun, which is a period of 365 days".[31]

Considering the meanings of all of these words in context and recalling that God is setting a pattern of order, it is now understood that the second purpose of lights was setting in order the celebration of Holy Days!

You see, the terms *signs, seasons, days* and *years* refer to the sun and moon being used to communicate or signal an event. They are used in calculating the times of observance of Holy Days based on the rising of the sun. Consider the Hebrew Calendar where the sun and the moon play a significant role in determining the exact date of sacred feasts, sabbath days and assemblies for the children of Israel and the people of God. Although humankind had not yet been created, God was setting a pattern of set times for them to meet with Him. Time revealed through the activity of the sun and the moon were designed to assist God's people in knowing when to meet with him. You see, God is a relational God. If you are familiar with the journey of the children of Israel out of Egypt and heading toward the land of promise, you know that God instructed Moses to build a Tent of Meeting which is later called the Tent of Congregation or Tabernacle. This Tent of Meeting was a movable dwelling place for God's presence and the place to inquire of God. Ultimately, it was a place of worship.

God instituted specific days that were to be set apart (holy) for His people to spend with Him. It is here, at the Tent of Meeting, that the people of God were to come and meet and worship Him. Let's look at some of the Holy Days and their respective time of celebration as mentioned in scripture:

Sabbath Day - the day of rest for people and animals. The Sabbath day was to occur every 7th *day.* (Exodus 20: 8-11, 31:12-17; Leviticus 23:3; Deuteronomy 5:12-15)

Sabbath Year - the year of rest for the land, people and animals. The Sabbath Year was to occur every 7th *year.* (Exodus 23:10-11; Leviticus 25:1-7)

Year of Jubilee - the year of canceled debts, freeing of slaves and indentured servants. Additionally, land was to be returned to the original family owners. The Year of Jubilee occurs every *50*th *year.* (Leviticus 25:8-55; 27:17-24; Numbers 36:4)

Feast of Passover - the time to remember when God delivered the children of Israel from bondage in Egypt. This feast occurs the *1*st *month, 14*th *day of each year.* (Exodus 12:1-14; Leviticus 23:5; Numbers 9:1-14; 28:16; Deuteronomy 16:1-7)

Feast of Unleavened Bread - the time for the children of Israel to remember how the Lord brought them out of Egypt quickly. This feast occurs the *1*st *month, 15*th*-21*st *day of the year.* (Exodus 12:15-20; 13:3-10; 23:15; 34:18; Leviticus 23:6-8; Numbers 28:17; Deuteronomy 16:3-4,8)

First Fruits - the time for the children of Israel to recognize the Lord's abundance in the land. First Fruits is celebrated in the *1*st *month on the 16*th *day of each year.* (Leviticus 23:9-14)

Pentecost also referred to as the Feast of Weeks - is about showing thankfulness for the Lord's blessing of harvest. Pentecost is a feast of joy and encompasses mandatory and voluntary offerings to God including the first fruits of the wheat harvest. This feast is celebrated in the *3*rd *month on the 6*th *day of the year.* (Exodus 23:16; 34:22; Leviticus 23:15-21; Numbers 28:26-31; Deuteronomy 16:9-12)

Feast of Trumpets also referred to as Rosh Ha-shanah - an assembly commemorated with blowing the shofar, sacrifices and presenting the Israelites before the Lord for His favor. This assembly occurs in the *7th month, 1st day of each year.* (Leviticus 23:23-25; Numbers 29:1-6)

Day of Atonement also called Yom Kippur - a day of rest, fasting and sacrifices for cleansing the priests and people from their sins as well as purification for the Holy Place. This assembly occurred in the *7th month, 10th day of each year.* (Leviticus 16; 23:26-31; Numbers 29:7-11)

Feast of Tabernacles also referred to as the Feast of Booths - a seven day celebration designed to cause the Israelites to remember their journey from Egypt to Canaan. It is also a time to give thanks to God for the productivity of the promised land. This celebration takes place in the *7th month, 15th-21st day.* (Exodus 23:16; 34:22; Leviticus 23:33-36, 39-43; Numbers 29:12-34; Deuteronomy 16:13-15; Zechariah 14:16-19)

Purim - a day of feasting to remind the Jews of their survival and national deliverance in the time of Queen Esther. It is a day of joy and exchanging presents. This feast takes place in the *12th month, 14th -15th day.* (Esther 9:18-32)

The aforementioned Holy Days, sacred assemblies and feasts were directly related to the children of Israel having set times with God based on the revolution of time. Many of which were for remembrance or sacrifice.

What is ~~Day 4~~/ the 4th setting of order really about?

- The light that God spoke on day 1, was to be placed in the world in the midst of the waters and was to rule **in** the world to set order of moral versus immoral activity according to the righteousness of God which was among, but separate from, the darkness. Alternatively, the lights (sun, moon, planets, and stars) were to rule in the firmament of the heaven and provide a light source **for and upon** the earth.

- The 4th setting of order is also the institution of time. God is setting the pattern or setting the order of **time**. The lights (sun, moon, planets, and stars) is God instituting time determined by the rising and setting of the sun!

Again we see that The Creation is about God setting order for the earthly realm:

~~Day 1~~ - 1st setting of order:
Establishing what is good (moral activity) based on what God determines - setting the pattern of good/moral versus immoral.

~~Day 2~~ - 2nd setting of order:
Setting the pattern of the earthly realm in the midst of the spiritual realm.

~~Day 3~~ - 3rd setting of order:

Setting the pattern of reproduction for the earthly realm.

~~Day 4~~ - 4th setting of order:

Setting the pattern of time for the earthly realm.

~~DAY 5~~ - 5ᵀᴴ SETTING OF ORDER

And God said, Let the waters bring forth abundantly the moving creature that hath life, and fowl that may fly above the earth in the open firmament of heaven.

And God created great whales, and every living creature that moveth, which the waters brought forth abundantly, after their kind, and every winged fowl after his kind: and God saw that it was good.

And God blessed them, saying, Be fruitful, and multiply, and fill the waters in the seas, and let fowl multiply in the earth.

And the evening and the morning were the fifth day.

Genesis 1:20-23

49

WATER CREATURE AND FOWL

As far back as I can remember, I was taught that God created all animals on day 5 and created man on day 6. However, Genesis 1:20-23 reveals something different. In the aforementioned scriptures, God specifically commands the waters to bring forth two kinds of creatures:

1. the moving creature that has life

2. the fowl that may fly above the earth

What did God bring forth? He brought forth the moving creature and fowl that fly, not ALL animals!

Let's look at these scriptures a bit closer and examine what God did in the 5th setting of order. I will start our discussion with the creation of the fowl.

FOWL THAT MAY FLY ABOVE THE EARTH

Genesis 1:20 indicates that God said, "Let the waters bring forth abundantly the moving creature that hath life, and fowl that may fly above the earth in the open firmament of heaven."

There are two areas that I would like to examine:

1. Every winged fowl that flies above the earth, and

2. How God blessed the fowl by telling them to be fruitful and multiply on the earth.

Before I dissect these two areas, I think we need to understand what fowl are in this context.

The word *fowl* is defined as "flying creatures, fowl, insects, birds".[32]

We see here that God created all species of fowl, birds and insects that have the capability of flying above the waters. He also blessed them and commanded them to multiply on the earth.

Consider our scripture...

What did God create? *Fowl that fly.*

Where did they fly? *Above the earth, in the sky.*

Where were they to multiply? *On the earth.*

Scripture discusses God creating fowl that fly but what about the fowl, birds and insects that don't? While birds are known for their ability to fly, there are many that do not fly such as penguins, ostriches, and kiwis. Where do these kinds of birds fit in? Where do insects that don't fly like fleas and head lice fit in? These were also created, but not in the 5th setting of order. We will discuss these species of fowl a little later.

MOVING CREATURE

Referring back to our scripture, Genesis 1:20, we see that the waters were also to bring forth the moving creature.

As usual, I would like to define the term moving creature and the definition that is in context with our text is highlighted.

Moving creature is defined as "**breath, soul, living being, life**, self, person, desire, passion, appetite, emotion".[33]

Verse 21 provides more information stating that these souls are "the great whales and every living creature that moveth in the waters".

The word *whales* is defined as "a marine or land monster, i.e. sea-serpent or jackal; dragon, sea-monster, serpent or whale[34] and refers to elongated or any other huge marine animal".[35]

What did God create? Sea serpent, dragon, whales and all kinds of fish.

Where were they to fill? *In the waters in the Seas.*

"God blessed the moving creature telling them to be fruitful, multiply and fill the waters in the seas". Why did God specifically command the water creatures to fill 'the seas' and not to fill 'the waters'? The answer is fairly simple.

> God didn't instruct the moving creature to fill the waters because there were also waters above the firmament!

Can you imagine walking around on earth and seeing elongated sea monsters or whales floating around over your head? I'm not sure I would be comfortable with that activity. God was clear in indicating where He wanted the moving creature to dwell - IN THE SEAS.

In blessing the moving creature, God showed His approval and told them to bear fruit and increase in number. Essentially, God is commanding the moving creature to reproduce. What God created in the 5th setting of order is what humans commonly refer to now as birds and marine animals.

If you recall, in Genesis 1:2, in the 1st setting of order, there were all waters which the Spirit of God moved upon and there was darkness and deep. Then God puts a firmament in the midst of the waters and moves some of the waters up and some down. Then, the waters that were down, He gathered them together unto one place and called them *Seas*. There is a clear distinction between *waters* and *seas*, shown also in God's instruction of where the marine animals were to live.

Waters were on earth as well as above the firmament and the Spirit of God moved upon the face of them all. However, seas directly referred to the waters gathered below on earth.

Why is that important?

According to Genesis 1:20, where did the moving creature and fowl come from? They came from the *waters*! When God said let the waters bring forth, one of three things occurred:

- Either the waters *above* brought forth the fowl and the waters *below* brought forth the moving creature.

- The waters *below* brought forth the fowl *and* the moving creature.

- The waters *above* brought forth fowl and the moving creature.

Whichever scenario or whichever of the waters brought them forth, they all came from waters.

Up to this point, nothing seems too out of the ordinary, except one thing.

My question in the previous paragraph was asking how the waters brought forth the moving creature, living creature and fowl.

In other words, how did the *waters bring forth souls and life*?

Recall in day 1 or the 1st setting of order, God said "let there be light" and it was revealed that God didn't have to create light, He just gave what was already in Him? He didn't make it. He didn't create it. He said it.

Let me refresh your memory by reviewing what God did in 'setting order' as shown in Genesis 1.

~~Day 1~~ - 1ˢᵗ setting of order:
 Light - God said, God saw and God called

~~Day 2~~ - 2ⁿᵈ setting of order:
 Heaven, Earth and Seas - God said, God **made**, God called and God saw

~~Day 3~~ - 3ʳᵈ setting of order:
 Vegetation - God said and God saw

~~Day 4~~ - 4ᵗʰ setting of order:
 Lights - God said, God **made**, God set and God saw

~~Day 5~~ - 5ᵗʰ setting of order:
 Fowl and Marine Animals - God said, God **created** and God blessed

There are two words that I would like to define (again paying close attention to the highlighted contextual meanings).

The word *made* means "to make, to be done **(from something)**".[36]

The word *created* means "to create, Creator, to be created can refer to creating **from nothing**".[37]

Now, recall Genesis 1:20-22 paying close attention to the highlighted text.

 *And **God said, Let the waters bring***

> *forth* abundantly the moving creature **that hath life**, and fowl that may fly above the earth in the open firmament of heaven.
>
> And **God created** great whales, and **every living creature that moveth**, which the waters brought forth abundantly, after their kind, and every winged fowl after his kind: and God saw that it was good.
>
> And **God blessed** them, saying, Be fruitful, and multiply, and fill the waters in the seas, and let fowl multiply in the earth.

Did you notice anything?

The 5th setting of order is God creating. Creating something from nothing. This is the first thing that God created! Prior to this, God said, God called, and God made. This time, God said and God created. Then God blessed what He created. This is the first time God created souls. This is the first time God created life and because they are alive, because they have life, they can be blessed to reproduce life. Do you see that connection?

We see that God is now adding life to the firmament He called Heaven and to the world - all within the earthly realm. Recall, the vegetation was not considered life. Vegetation was not mentioned as having a soul, vegetation was mentioned as having a seed.

That all sounds good, but my question still remains...The question was: How did the waters bring forth souls and life?

LIFE FROM THE WATERS

In order to provide clarity, it would be beneficial to review a portion of the 1st succession of order formerly referred to as day 1.

Genesis 1:1-2 reads (*emphasis added*):

In the beginning God created the heaven and the earth.

And the earth was without form, and void; and darkness was upon the face of the deep. ***And the Spirit of God moved upon the face of the waters.***

Focusing on the latter part of verse 2, let's define a few more words.

The word *Spirit* is defined as "wind, breath".[38]

The word *moved*, as we learned in the 1st setting of order, means to "tremble, shake, hover".[7]

Considering these definitions with the highlighted portion of Genesis 1:2, a question comes to mind. If the Spirit of God trembled or shook the waters, then the Spirit of God has dominion over the waters. Just as darkness had dominion over the deep, defined as "the abode of the dead". We know that the Spirit of God affected the waters, but what does that have to do with fowl, birds and marine animals being created from the waters? Several passages of scripture can help us answer this question.

59

So is this great and wide sea, wherein are things creeping innumerable, both small and great beasts.

There go the ships: there is that leviathan, whom thou hast made to play therein.

These wait all upon thee; that thou mayest give them their meat in due season.

That thou givest them they gather: thou openest thine hand, they are filled with good.

Thou hidest thy face, they are troubled: thou takest away their breath, they die, and return to their dust.

***Thou sendest forth thy spirit, they are created:** and thou renewest the face of the earth.*

Psalm 104:25-30, emphasis added

*By the word of the Lord were the heavens made; and **all the host of them by the breath of his mouth.***

Psalm 33:6, emphasis added

*The spirit of God hath made me, and **the breath of the Almighty hath given me life**.*

Job 33:4, emphasis added

Now the birth of Jesus Christ was on this wise: When as his mother Mary was es-

*poused to Joseph, before they came togeth-
er, she was found **with child of the Holy
Ghost**.*

Matthew 1:18, emphasis added

Did you notice any similarities in the highlighted text?

According to the aforementioned scriptures, the Spirit of God is LIFE! What did the waters bring forth? Moving creature that have LIFE and those LIVING creatures. It is by the Spirit of God - His breath, that brought forth life from the waters. It is by the Spirit of God that life was given to what God created by speaking!

It is now understood that in the 5th setting of order, God has commanded the waters, which were already present before the firmament, the world and the seas were created, to produce something. The Spirit of God that dominated the waters caused the waters to produce life and God saw that it was good (moral and pleasing). He was pleased with the new order, the pattern that He had set in place. And evening and morning were the 5th day!

Nothing else prior to the 5th setting of order *received the blessing of God.*

Nothing else prior to the 5th setting of order was *commanded to reproduce and increase.*

Nothing else prior to the 5th setting of order had been *given a soul.*

Nothing else prior to the 5th setting of order had been *given life.*

The 5th setting of order is the introduction of souls and life as well as the introduction of blessings to reproduce.

The 5th setting of order - going from chaos to order - is to bring forth life in the waters and in the firmament as well as bringing forth the pattern of the reproduction of life! We see "water animal lives and souls" being created.

Setting of Order

~~Day 1~~ - 1st setting of order:
> Establishing what is good (moral activity) based on what God determines - setting the pattern of good/moral versus immoral.

~~Day 2~~ - 2nd setting of order:
> Setting the pattern of the earthly realm in the midst of the spiritual realm.

~~Day 3~~ - 3rd setting of order:
> Setting the pattern of reproduction for the earth realm.

~~Day 4~~ - 4th setting of order:
> Setting the pattern of time for the earth realm.

~~Day 5~~ - 5th setting of order:
> Setting the pattern of souls and life of water and flying animals as well as the introduction of blessings to reproduce.

~~DAY 6~~ - 6TH SETTING OF ORDER

═══════════════════════════

And God said, Let the earth bring forth the living creature after his kind, cattle, and creeping thing, and beast of the earth after his kind: and it was so.

And God made the beast of the earth after his kind, and cattle after their kind, and every thing that creepeth upon the earth after his kind: and God saw that it was good.

And God said, Let us make man in our image, after our likeness: and let them have dominion over the fish of the sea, and over the fowl of the air, and over the cattle, and over all the earth, and over every creeping thing that creepeth upon the earth.

So God created man in his own image, in the image of God created he, him; male and female created he, them.

And God blessed them, and God said unto them, Be fruitful, and multiply, and replenish the earth, and subdue it: and have dominion over the fish of the sea, and over the fowl of the air, and over every living thing that moveth upon the earth.

And God said, Behold, I have given you every herb bearing seed, which is upon the face of all the earth, and every tree, in the which is the fruit of a tree yielding seed; to you it shall be for meat.

And to every beast of the earth, and to every fowl of the air, and to every thing that creepeth upon the earth, wherein there is life, I have given every green herb for meat: and it was so.

And God saw every thing that he had made, and, behold, it was very good. And the evening and the morning were the sixth day.

Genesis 1:24-31

LAND ANIMALS AND MAN

I t is now the 6ᵗʰ setting of order and according to Genesis 1:24-31, God performs two things:

1. Makes land animals

2. Creates man

We discovered in the previous chapter, in the 5ᵗʰ setting of order formerly called day 5, that God commanded the *waters* to bring forth the living creature to fill the firmament and to multiply in the seas. Now, in the 6ᵗʰ setting of order previously called day 6, we see God commanding the *earth* to bring forth. God commands what He created to create something again! God commands the earth to bring forth the living creature that moves on the earth.

Did you notice in the 5th setting of order as stated in Genesis 1:20, that God created the moving creature, the living creature **from the waters**. While here in the 6th setting of order as stated in Genesis 1:24, God created the living creature **from the earth**? The term *living creature* is defined as "life, state of living, flesh".[39]

According to Genesis 1:24-31, there are two categories of the living creature of the earth that were created in the 6th setting of order.

1. Beast, cattle and creeping thing

2. Man

BEAST, CATTLE AND CREEPING THING

Genesis 1:24-25 states that God said,

> *"Let the earth bring forth the living creature after his kind, cattle, and creeping thing, and beast of the earth after his kind: and it was so."*

And God made the beast of the earth after his kind, and cattle after their kind, and every thing that creepeth upon the earth after his kind: and God saw that it was good.

The Bible indicates that these animals were *made*, not *created*. Recall, the meaning of the word *made* means "to make, to be done **(from something)** to do, fashion, accomplish".[36]

Genesis 1:24-25 tells us that God has commanded the earth to bring forth all land animals, beast, cattle and those that creep along the ground. These would include lions, tigers, bears, (oh my), kangaroos, dogs, cats, cows, bulls, sheep, rabbits, moles, squirrels, opossum etc. as well as fowl and insects that do not fly but walk the earth (as discussed in the 5th setting of order) including worms, grasshoppers, ants, spiders, lice, fleas, etc....and God said it was good.

I must admit that prior to studying The Creation, I never considered all the species of land animals and insects that were running around on the earth in the beginning. I had only considered the larger animals. This now causes me to ponder if insects were also on Noah's Ark. It is always a great time to reflect on what you thought you knew about The Creation and begin to go deeper into what God intended with each day He created and why.

Let's continue dissecting the remainder of the 6th succession of order - the creation of man.

MAN

Advancing into the 6th setting of order we discover that in Genesis 1:26-31, God is discussing the creation of man.

The word *man* is defined as "humankind, both male and female".[40] With this definition in mind, I will use the term *man* when referring to human beings, regardless of gender.

The text states that God created man but He doesn't create man like He has made the other animals in the 6th setting of order, nor does God create man in the same manner He has made or created anything else from the 2nd through the 5th setting of order. This time God does something different.

Now, I know many of you have heard about man being created but lean into what God is revealing here. God is going to reveal something I'm sure you haven't previously heard.

I am going to spend the remainder of this book discussing the man that God created and, to do so, I am going to have to look at a few more scriptures outside of the first chapter of Genesis to help us gain better understanding. Therefore, I will be discussing text from the balance of Genesis 1 and will also probe into Genesis 2. I am interjecting one scripture from the second chapter of Genesis within Genesis 1:26-29 as shown below to help understand what took place when God created man.

And God said, Let us make man in our image, after our likeness: and let them have dominion over the fish of the sea, and over the fowl of the air, and over the cattle, and over all the earth, and over every creeping thing that creepeth upon the earth.

Genesis 1:26

So God created man in his own image, in the image of God created he, him; male and female created he, them.

Genesis 1:27

And the Lord God formed man of the dust of the ground, and breathed into his nostrils the breath of life; and man became a living soul.

Genesis 2:7

And God blessed them, and God said unto them, Be fruitful, and multiply, and replenish the earth, and subdue it: and have dominion over the fish of the sea, and over the fowl of the air, and over every living thing that moveth upon the earth.

Genesis 1:28

And God said, Behold, I have given you every herb bearing seed, which is upon the face of all the earth, and every tree, in the which is the fruit of a tree yielding seed; to you it shall be for meat.

Genesis 1:29

IMAGE

Recall God has already created flesh in fish, birds, beast, cattle and creeping things; however, when He creates man, He changes course. 1 Corinthians 15:39 states:

> *All flesh is not the same flesh: but there is one*
> *kind of flesh of men, another flesh of beasts,*
> *another of fishes, and another of birds.*

Note that each life that God created or made from the waters and the earth have the capacity to reproduce. Additionally, every living thing God has created thus far is after his or their kind yet, when God discusses making man, He said,

> "Let **us** make man in our image and after
> our likeness".

God's newest creation is making man and now God is making man after another kind, after the kind that God refers to as "Us" in Genesis 1:26.

Additionally, everything that was made or created thus far, scripture says God did it. But, when man is proposed, it is "Us" that is making him.

Now, as I state in my livestream teachings at Illumination Kingdom Teachings on YouTube, the Hebrew word for God is *Elohim*. Elohim is used as the general name for God, the Creator. The name *Elohim* is plural in form, but singular in meaning. God being three persons, plural in form but still one person, thereby singular in meaning. With that understanding, who is the "Us" that God commissioned to make man? Who is the plurality of God, Elohim, The Creator? To understand who is being referred to as "Us", we need to dig a little deeper.

God had determined that He wants man to be made in the image and after the likeness of someone He refers to as "Us". In order to understand, it's ideal to first look at the image and the likeness in the characteristics of which man will be made.

When most people read *"And God created man in his own image"* they develop a mental picture of the appearance of human beings and then attribute this image to God. They are reasoning that if man is made in the image of God, then God must resemble humans, but John 4:24 states that God is a Spirit.

If God is a Spirit and, according to Genesis 2:7, humans are in natural or earthly bodies, then we need to understand man being created in the image and after the likeness of God.

Let's look at this a little closer:

The word *create* has a two fold meaning. "It means to create from nothing and it also means to be fat or to fill."[36] In this context, the word *create* does not mean to create from nothing as was indicated in day 5 (5th setting of order), instead creating life in day 6 (6th setting of order) is different, because Genesis 2:7 states that God is creating out of something here - He has earth and He has "Us" to create from.

73

Genesis 2:7 further states that God "formed" man. The word *formed* is defined as "the process of pressing clay together to form an object such as a figurine".[41] It is evident from this verse that man was made from something. Therefore, in this context, the second meaning of the word create "to be fat" or "to be filled" applies.

Continuing to dissect how "Us" is making man, we need to define the word *image,* which is "an outline of a shadow, a representation or image of the original."[42]

Considering the aforementioned definitions, when speaking of the image and after the likeness of what God calls "Us", it is discovered that Genesis 1:26-27 really reads as follows:

> *And God said, Let us **fatten or fill man with a representation of Us, and fatten or fill him** after our likeness: and let them have dominion over the fish of the sea, and over the fowl of the air, and over the cattle, and over all the earth, and over every creeping thing that creepeth upon the earth.*
>
> *So God **fattened or filled man in the representation of Himself,** in the **representation** of God **fattened or filled** He him; male and female **fattened or filled** He them.*

> Being made in the image of God is not refer-
> ring to the physical appearance, but more
> directly to what man will **_do_** and how man
> will **_function_**.

God fattened or filled within man a pattern, a representation of God's own functions: creativity, purpose, thought,
dominion, holiness and morality, to name a few.

Additionally, Genesis 1:28-29 indicates that God is giving
man several things, it reads:

> *Be fruitful, and multiply, and replenish the
> earth, and subdue it: and have dominion
> over the fish of the sea, and over the fowl
> of the air, and over every living thing that
> moveth upon the earth.*

> *And God said, Behold, I have given you ev-
> ery herb bearing seed, which is upon the
> face of all the earth, and every tree, in the
> which is the fruit of a tree yielding seed; to
> you it shall be for meat.*

Not only has God made man in His image, He also gave
them:

- Reproduction
- Authority
- Dominion
- Provision

If God gave these attributes, then God holds the sovereignty to give and God has given man the same functions as Him if man is fattened or filled with His representation. God has now begun to make the pattern of man among all the order that was set prior to man being created.

What then is the representation that man was fattened or filled with? Let's define representation.

Representation is...

- "the action of speaking or acting on behalf of someone

- the description or portrayal of someone or something in a particular way or as being of a certain nature."[43]

That tells us that the biblical representation of God's use of "Us" for man as fattened or filled with means having the **function** to speak, portray, and act on the behalf of "Us" in the territory that God has placed man. Having the function to portray "Us" in a place that "Us" puts this man.

Thus the image of man is the express representation of those that created him. Man has been given the function to act and speak on behalf of those that created him, the authority to portray those who God referred to as "Us". God created "image bearers" in humans, but Genesis 1:26 didn't say that man was made only "in our image" but man was made "in our image, after our likeness".

> *And God said, Let us make man in our image, after our likeness: and let them have*

76

*dominion over the fish of the sea, and over
the fowl of the air, and over the cattle, and
over all the earth, and over every creeping
thing that creepeth upon the earth.*

Image and after the likeness are not synonymous; they are two separate things. It has been explained that image is the representation of someone; acting or speaking on their behalf, portraying someone, while likeness is different. Let's explore this in our next section.

LIKENESS

The discussion of man being created in the image of God from the beginning, is an important foundation to understand scripture; however, I've only touched the surface of the creation of man because God also creates man after His likeness and God is still setting order, even with the creation of man.

The word *likeness* is defined as "figure, form or similitude which refers to the external, public display of something."[44] Ideally, likeness is something that looks close to the original, but is not exactly the same.

Likeness deals with the external view of something. In this context, it refers to the characteristics of "Us" that are presented to others. Therefore, if man is made after the likeness or after the characteristics of "Us", that reveals that man is almost the same as "Us", but not quite like them.

Let's read through a few passages of scripture to understand more.

Consider Joseph, the highly favored son of Jacob who gave Joseph a coat of many colors. Joseph who was hated by his brothers, cast into a pit, sold into slavery, and eventually thrown into prison due to false accusations. Then one day, Joseph interprets a dream of Pharaoh and provides some wise instructions based on said dream. The following passage of scripture reveals what happened next.

And Pharaoh said unto his servants, Can we find such a one as this is, a man in whom the Spirit of God is?

And Pharaoh said unto Joseph, Forasmuch as God hath shewed thee all this, there is none so discreet and wise as thou art:

Thou shalt be over my house, and according unto thy word shall all my people be ruled: only in the throne will I be greater than thou.

And Pharaoh said unto Joseph, See, I have set thee over all the land of Egypt.

And Pharaoh took off his ring from his hand, and put it upon Joseph's hand, and arrayed him in vestures of fine linen, and put a gold chain about his neck;

And he made him to ride in the second chariot which he had; and they cried before him, Bow the knee: and he made him ruler over all the land of Egypt.

And Pharaoh said unto Joseph, I am Pharaoh, and without thee shall no man lift up his hand or foot in all the land of Egypt.

Genesis 41:38-44

What did you see in this passage of scripture?

You see a person, who has the Spirit of God, being given a position of high rank, but still was not higher than the one that granted the rank. Joseph was given distinction with all authority and honor in Egypt above all people, but he was still subject to Pharaoh who maintained his kingly position. Joseph was made to be after the likeness of Pharaoh and given every external distinction of rulership that Pharaoh possessed, except Joseph wasn't Pharaoh or greater than Pharoah.

Likeness refers to a person that has every external characteristic of the giver, but just shy of being the giver himself. It refers to **position**.

Let's review to help you understand *distinction*, which is defined as:

- "a difference or contrast between similar things or people".
- "excellence that sets someone or something apart from others".[45]

Now that you can ascertain the difference between *image* and *after the likeness*, there is one more passage of scripture that will help you absorb what it means for man to be made in the image of "Us" and after their likeness.

King David said in Psalm 8 verses 3-6:

> *When I consider thy heavens, the work of thy fingers, the moon and the stars, which thou hast ordained;*
>
> *What is man, that thou art mindful of him? and the son of man, that thou visitest him?*

For thou hast made him a little lower than the angels and hast crowned him with glory and honour.

Thou madest him to have dominion over the works of thy hands; thou hast put all things under his feet:

Ironically, this scripture references what happened in the beginning when God initially made man - the very concept I am discussing in this book. Psalm 8 reveals that God has made man a little lower than the angels **and** has crowned him with glory and honour. Being 'a little lower than the angels' alludes to the *image/representation*; 'crowned with glory and honor' refers to *likeness/position*.

Once again, I would like to expound on a few words to bring more clarity to these scriptures.

The word *lower* means "to withhold, to deprive, to cause to lack".[46]

The word *angel* is the Hebrew word Elohim which, as stated previously, is defined as "God, plural of majesty with focus on great power; any person characterized by great power".[47]

Crowned means to "surround, close in upon, to bestow".[48]

Glory refers to "honor, splendor, wealth and high status".[49]

The word *honour* is defined as "majesty, splendor, glory, mobility - often related to an object that is beautiful and evokes awe".[50]

When these definitions are inserted in Psalm 8:5, it reads...

> *For thou hast made humankind a small lacking than God and have surrounded him with magnificence, great beauty, high status, splendor, honor, majesty and awe.*

This means that man was created to be like God but not God! They were made to portray "Us" with the action of speaking on the behalf of "Us" as well as having the characteristics of deity, magnificence, splendor, majesty, something to be awed: but lower than the position of "Us".

Let's review.

Remember, God is a spirit. When God made man in the image and after His likeness, man (both male and female) were created a spirit and He created them with authority as well as characteristics of magnificence, glory, honor, majesty and awe above everything that He made or created in the earthly realm.

You should now understand that the phrase "in our image and after our likeness" is referring to man being filled with the representation of this "Us" that God has commissioned to make man, thereby making man fully in spirit, patterned after representations of the authority, deity and majesty of "Us". Therein lies the difference between *function* and *position*.

This is how they vary:

Function/Image - A characteristic or quality of a thing

- that is what you've been given the authority to do and possess. This is used as a means of *function* and what you can do because of God.

Position/Likeness - A distinguishing feature of a person or thing from every other living thing, which is a means of *position* and who you are because of what God gave to man of Himself.

Why did God do this? Why make man a spirit and give them these functions and characteristics? Why make man like Them? God was setting order. He created another pattern. God made man spirit so that "Us" could have a relationship with them.

FORMED

God did not simply say, " let's make man in our image and after our likeness", but scripture indicates that God performed something else.

Genesis 2:7 states:

> And the Lord God formed man of the dust of the ground, and breathed into his nostrils the breath of life; and man became a living soul.

The Bible reveals that the Lord God then formed man. What is the difference between created (fattened or filled) and formed? Why would God *fatten* or *fill* man, then *form* man?

It has already been discovered that God made man a spirit with authority to act and speak on His behalf as well as patterned after His characteristics of majesty, glory, honor and awe. We also went over how God created man a spirit, in the spiritual realm. The forming of man was different. Therefore, man (male and female) was made a spiritual being **first** before the human being was formed!

Let's discuss the forming of man.

The word *formed* refers to squeezing into a shape. Thus, when the Lord God formed man, it was the process of pressing clay together to form an object like molding a figurine.

The Lord God is like a potter, forming man by pressing or squeezing together the soil and clay of the ground and other elements of the earth to form and shape an object in the earthly realm. The forming of man becomes the natural body - the flesh, bones, brain, organs, veins, cells, and everything that makes up the human body, which was also formed by "Us". They formed something to create the representation and pattern of Themselves by forming a body to be a vessel.

Why? So that this body, this vessel, could hold the spiritual representation, pattern and function of "Us" in the earthly realm - in the place that God has created to bring from chaos to order.

Before we were formed, man was first created a spirit, within the spiritual realm. "Us" then prepared and formed an earthly body to carry the representation of Themselves.

Coincidentally, did not the Word/Jesus have a body prepared for Him?

Hebrews 10:5 reads:

> *Wherefore when he cometh into the world,*
> *he saith, Sacrifice and offering thou wouldest*
> *not, but a body hast thou prepared me*:

Whether you believe that this scripture is referring figuratively to the Body of Christ or literally as Mary's womb, the vessel, a body, had to be prepared for Jesus to operate in the earth for the purpose of God to be accomplished.

> The only difference between Jesus and hu-
> mankind, as believers, is that we are made
> in the image after the likeness of God, but
> Jesus *is* God. He is not made in God's image
> or after God's likeness. He *is* God!

If you are following me, then you understand that before the Lord God formed man's body, man (male and female) were already made spiritually! The spirit of man had form before the body of man was made.

Jeremiah 1:5 provides confirmation. It reads:

> *Before I formed thee in the belly I knew thee; and before thou camest forth out of the womb I sanctified thee, and I ordained thee a prophet unto the nations.*

Knew, in this context, refers to having a relationship. This tells us that God had a relationship with Jeremiah, and with you, prior to anyone being formed on the earth.

Therefore, man is not determined by the body, because man was made spirit first. The body is merely a vessel to carry the representation and pattern, the characteristics of "Us". When the body passes away, the spirit still exists as it did before the body was formed. Thus your spiritual being is the core foundation of being human. God chose this pattern of humans so that man could relate to Him and have a relationship with Him, spiritually. Man was given godly abilities and characteristics without a physical body, solidifying that the spirit is the material part and higher nature of a human being - not the body, which is merely the vessel.

THE BREATH, THE NOSTRILS
AND
THE SOUL

One might think that the creation and forming of man was no small feat, but then God does something else. Genesis 2:7 reveals what occurred next.

> *And the Lord God formed man of the dust of the ground, and breathed into his nostrils the breath of life; and man became a living soul.*

As previously discussed, man was already filled with the representation of "Us" and patterned after their deity, living in the spiritual realm. The body was a prepared dirt vessel without function in the earthly realm. Scripture reveals that the Lord God breathed into the nostrils of the formed shape (physical body) and man became a *living soul* on earth. Without the breath of God, it was not a living soul as it is the breath of God that causes souls to come to life.

Let's shift our focus momentarily to The Breath, The Nostrils and The Soul as referenced in the above scripture, beginning with a few definitions.

THE BREATH

If the Lord God breathed or blew, then what He did was transfer a mass of air from Him into this formed clay shape. The breath the Lord God breathed into man's nostrils was not like blowing out a candle. He released *The Breath* that moves and empowers life. The Lord God breathed His air, His life-giving wind, His life force into the nostrils of man.

Why would God - in all His infinite wisdom and all the order and pattern that He is setting - determine that the best place to release His life - giving breath of power was in the nostrils of some shaped clay? He unfolded His rationale through scripture.

When the Lord God formed the body shape of man, everything needed for man to function: the brain, organs, veins, cells etc., was also created for the body - except the breath of life. The body was simply the vessel. Let's look at the access point to see why God used the nostrils to bring forth life.

THE NOSTRILS

Notice the Bible didn't say nose, it said nostrils. What's the difference? The human nose is the most protruding part of the face. The nose bears the first organ of the respiratory system in the body and it also contains the nostrils. The nostrils are the two holes of the nose which is the passageway for air and carries oxygen to the lungs.

If oxygen is what God is breathing into human beings, why not use the mouth? It's bigger, more room, and has more capacity. Both the nose and mouth provide avenues to the throat, which carries oxygen into the lungs. So, why not just use the mouth?

Simple - bigger isn't always better. Sorry, Texas!

Indulge me for a moment and take a deep breath through your nose. Exhale. Now, take a breath through your mouth. Did you notice the difference? When you breathe through your nose, you inhale more oxygen compared to what you take in when you breathe through your mouth.

Kathryn Carter, a Professor at Southern Illinois University - Edwardsville, explained to me that breathing through your nose carries up to 90% of the oxygen that your body needs to support your organs, tissues, and cells. Breathing through your nose allows you to take deeper breaths, which engages your lungs. When the lungs become active, they pump out more oxygen to the rest of the body namely the circulatory and respiratory systems, into the arteries, and the heart etc. Oxygen helps send nerve signals and messages throughout the body and is needed for the body to survive. It is the oxygen that maintains all the components in the body, causing it to function.

When the Lord God's power of living breath was released into the nostrils, the soul of man became alive, awakening the heart, forming the skin and activating other vital functions in the body. That is why the Lord God breathed through the nostrils when forming man.

THE SOUL

We've talked about The Breath and The Nostrils, both which awakened the soul of the human being on earth.

So, what did God, by His power of breath, bring to life? The soul!

The soul is simply the enlivening of man. The soul is the immaterial part of a human which has the ability to control the body. When I say immaterial, I mean that it is not the primary part. The body had no function as it was just a vessel for man's spirit. It is the breath of God that empowered and activated the soul encompassed in an earthly vessel by giving it power to function and to live as human. It wasn't the body that was activated - it was the soul. Therefore, the soul is the connection to the earthly realm which operates through the body and the soul is how humans relate to other beings. The soul is the nature of *man*, it is the nature of the *human being*.

We see then, that when the forming of man took place, it was a shape made of soil and clay that was the earthly form of the human kind (not the water animal kind, the flying animal kind, or the beast, cattle and creeping thing kind).

Neither soul, breath, nor body is the core or foundation of what makes up who you are. The soul is the immaterial part of the *human being*. It is what moves the body, which is our human nature. It is the fundamental dispositions and characteristics of the way we think, feel, and respond - and the natural attributes that humans possess. The soul appeals to self. It is also how we connect with other humans and how we have relationships with one another.

When God formed this shape of man in the earth, He was forming man in their earthly/natural form. That tells us that when God said, "Let us make man", He was referring to making man, a kind of earthly being and began this project by creating man with a spirit *first*, then adding a living soul.

Let's clarify the difference.

The spirit of man is the connection to the spiritual realm, the soul is the connection to the earthly realm.

The spirit relates to God, the soul relates to humans (self included).

God created us with relationship in mind. He desires a relationship which can only be done via the spirit. Why? Because God is a Spirit thus He gave man a spirit to connect and relate to Him and to understand His ways, His will, and His desires. Man was created to function as a spirit, led by God, in the earthly realm.

The spirit is designed to interact with God spiritually and is concerned with spiritual things.

The soul is not spirit but earthly and therefore, by its nature, it relates to earthly things - the ways, will and desires of things on the earth. The soul is designed to interact with other humans on the earth.

The spirit is of the spirit nature, the nature of God, the

soul is of the human nature, the nature of the world.

The spirit is the material (primary) part of you, the soul is the immaterial (secondary) part of you.

Because God created the soul to be led by His Spirit and act through His will, the soul controls the body; however, the struggle of your soul is whether or not to act out God's will on the earth. This is one reason why the devil tempts the flesh by influencing the soul to give into our earthly human nature instead of allowing God's Spirit to influence us for good.

The *spirit* is the core of the spirit being, the spirit kind, the kind that God made in His image and after His likeness. The spirit is what guides you and is directly related to God.

The *soul* is the human kind, the human nature, more concerned with self - your mind, will, emotions, hopes, dreams, goals, and aspirations. Human nature desires to act out it's will through your soul.

The *body* is what carries it out on earth and how the spirit is manifested and how the soul relates to other souls in the earthly realm.

Therefore, you are a spirit being inside of a human being. Your spiritual nature is the truth and center of who you are. It is a deity and you carry the representation, function and power of God in the earthly realm.

I would like to show you this concept visually, so keep in mind that:

1. Everything I am discussing is prior to the fall of man, before Adam sinned and everything changed.

2. The body is simply a vehicle for the soul.

3. God is creating order for the earth and also for man.

Mankind was created as follows:

- The *body* following the soul
- The *soul* following the spirit
- The *spirit* following God

95

See, in the beginning, man was created as a spirit, formed a soul in a body to reign on the earth as representatives of God. God created the spirit to control the soul which is exhibited in a body that moves on earth.

Man was created so that...

- Whatever has dominance of the soul will control the body (whether spirit or flesh).

- The spirit, being the material part of man, should be what leads or influences man's soul.

- The body had no function except to be a vessel. It had no morality or immorality.

The body was not made for you and your pleasure, it was created for the will of "Us" on the earth. It was created to carry the representation, the portrayal and the deity of Them in the earthly realm. Take note that if representation and deity is the configuration that is like "Us", then "Us" must have these functions and characteristics as well.

I would like to remind you that everything God did up til now is to take things from chaos to order and the beginning was about God setting that pattern for order.

I have spent the last several chapters reviewing Genesis 1:26-31 and Genesis 2:7, looking intently at the making of man by "Us" along with several other concepts.

We learned that "Us" has:

1. *fattened or filled man in the **image** of "Us" with their: Spirit, Representation, Portrayal, and Function.*

2. *fattened or filled man **after the likeness** of "Us" by giving them: Deity, Position, and Distinction.*

3. *given man dominion over the fish of the sea, over the fowl of the air, over the cattle, over all the earth, and over every creeping thing that creepeth upon the earth.*

4. *formed man from the dirt, blew His life force into the dirt He shaped, and man became a living soul with the nature of a human being.*

5. *put the soul within a dirt shape revealing that the body and soul were not two different entities because it is when the soul came alive that the form became a body.*

6. *formed this human body to be a vessel, to carry man's spirit that God created on the earth. Additionally, the body was not formed for man's pleasure, but for the will and purpose of "Us", which was to be the representation and deity of Them in the earthly realm.*

I have expounded on how man was created, the transitional creation of man from a thought of God to becoming a spiritual being, and finally a human being.

With such a vast amount of information, you may have thought that what has been discussed thus far was the culmination of the creation of man, but there is more.

THE MOVE OF GOD

These are the generations of the heavens and of the earth when they were created, in the day that the Lord God made the earth and the heavens,

And every plant of the field before it was in the earth, and every herb of the field before it grew: for the Lord God had not caused it to rain upon the earth, and there was not a man to till the ground.

But there went up a mist from the earth, and watered the whole face of the ground.

And the Lord God formed man of the dust of the ground, and breathed into his nostrils the breath of life; and man became a living soul.

And the Lord God planted a garden eastward in Eden; and there he put the man whom he had formed.

And out of the ground made the Lord God to grow every tree that is pleasant to the sight, and good for food; the tree of life also in the

99

midst of the garden, and the tree of knowledge of good and evil.

Genesis 2:4-9

And the Lord God took the man, and put him into the garden of Eden to dress it and to keep it.

And the Lord God commanded the man, saying, Of every tree of the garden thou mayest freely eat:

But of the tree of the knowledge of good and evil, thou shalt not eat of it: for in the day that thou eatest thereof thou shalt surely die.

And the Lord God said, It is not good that the man should be alone; I will make a help meet for him.

And out of the ground the Lord God formed every beast of the field, and every fowl of the air; and brought them unto Adam to see what he would call them: and whatsoever Adam called every living creature, that was the name thereof.

And Adam gave names to all cattle, and to the fowl of the air, and to every beast of the field; but for Adam there was not found an help meet for him.

And the Lord God caused a deep sleep to fall

upon Adam, and he slept: and he took one of his ribs, and closed up the flesh instead thereof;

And the rib, which the Lord God had taken from man, made he a woman, and brought her unto the man.

And Adam said, This is now bone of my bones, and flesh of my flesh: she shall be called Woman, because she was taken out of Man.

Genesis 2:15-23

Before examining the "Move of God", we need to look closely at this passage of scripture in comparison to Genesis 1.

Genesis 2:4 explains the account of the heaven and earth *when* they were created. That tells us the information following Genesis 2:4 happened during The Creation, not after, and it is a more detailed account of what occurred. Let's conduct a quick review:

Setting of Order in Succession as revealed in Genesis 1:

~~Day 1~~ - 1st setting of order:
   Light - God said, God saw and God called

~~Day 2~~ - 2nd setting of order:
   Heaven, Earth and Seas - God said, God made, God called and God saw

101

~~Day 3~~ - 3rd setting of order:

    Vegetation - God said and God saw

~~Day 4~~ - 4th setting of order:

    Lights - God said, God made, God set and God saw

~~Day 5~~ - 5th setting of order:

    Fowl/Birds and Marine Animals - God said, God created and God blessed

~~Day 6~~ - 6th setting of order:

    Land Animals and Man - God said, God created, God blessed

God is the common factor. If **God** is credited for doing everything in Genesis 1, why is the **Lord God** credited as doing everything in Genesis 2? Let's review several abbreviated verses from Genesis 2.

> *...the **Lord God** made the earth and the heavens - Genesis 2:4, emphasis added*

> *...for the **Lord God** had not caused it to rain upon the earth - Genesis 2:5, emphasis added*

> *...the **Lord God** formed man of the dust of the ground - Genesis 2:7, emphasis added*

> *...the **Lord God** planted a garden eastward in Eden - Genesis 2:8, emphasis added*

> *...out of the ground made the **Lord God** to*

grow every tree that is pleasant to the sight - Genesis 2:9, emphasis added

*... the **Lord God** took the man, and put him into the garden of Eden to dress it and to keep it. - Genesis 2:15, emphasis added*

*...the **Lord God** commanded the man - Genesis 2:16, emphasis added*

*... the **Lord God** said, It is not good that the man should be alone - Genesis 2:18, emphasis added*

*... out of the ground the **Lord God** formed every beast of the field, and every fowl of the air - Genesis 2:19, emphasis added*

*... the **Lord God** caused a deep sleep to fall upon Adam, and he slept: and he took one of his ribs, and closed up the flesh instead thereof; - Genesis 2:21, emphasis added*

*... the rib, which the **Lord God** had taken from man, made he a woman, and brought her unto the man. - Genesis 2:22, emphasis added*

If Genesis 2 is additional detail of what happened in Genesis 1, then something else is going on. As I looked more intently, Holy Spirit began to show me more differences in the following text. Let's check out these differences and pay close attention to the highlighted words.

DIFFERENCES BETWEEN GENESIS 1 & GENESIS 2

Vegetation

And God said, Let the earth bring forth grass, the herb yielding seed, and the fruit tree yielding fruit after his kind, whose seed is in itself, upon the earth: and it was so.

And the **earth brought forth grass, and herb yielding seed after his kind, and the tree yielding fruit,** *whose seed was in itself, after his kind: and God saw that it was good.*

Genesis 1:11-12, emphasis added

These are the generations of the heavens and of the earth when they were created, in the day that the Lord God made the earth and the heavens,

And every **plant of the field** *before it was in the earth, and every* **herb of the field** *before it grew: for the Lord God had not caused it to rain upon the earth, and there was not a man to till the ground.*

Genesis 2:4-5, emphasis added

104

In Genesis 1, **grass, and herb yielding seed after his kind, and the tree yielding fruit** are stated as being created; however in Genesis 2, the Bible states the **plant of the field and herb of the field**. This is the first time we are seeing the words *plant and field*.

Beast

> *And God said, Let the earth bring forth the living creature after his kind, cattle, and creeping thing, and **beast of the earth** after his kind: and it was so.*
>
> *And God made the **beast of the earth** after his kind, and cattle after their kind, and every thing that creepeth upon the earth after his kind: and God saw that it was good.*
>
> Genesis 1:24-25, emphasis added

> *And out of the ground the Lord God formed every **beast of the field**, and every fowl of the air; and brought them unto Adam to see what he would call them: and whatsoever Adam called every living creature, that was the name thereof.*
>
> *And Adam gave names to all cattle, and to the fowl of the air, and to every **beast of the field**; but for Adam there was not found an help meet for him.*
>
> Genesis 2:19-20, emphasis added

105

In Genesis 1, the **beast of the earth** is stated as being created; however in Genesis 2, the Bible states the **beast of the field**. This is the first time we are seeing the term *beast of the field*.

Also, the fowl of the air in Genesis 1 came forth from the waters, and animals were made before man. However, Genesis 2, states that man was created first and then land animals?

Additionally, there is no mention of water animals in Genesis 2; therefore, the images that depict Adam speaking to animals coming out of the water in the Garden of Eden don't seem to be accurate as there was no mention of animals from the water in the Garden of Eden.

Man

> *And God said, Let us make man in our image, after our likeness: and let them have dominion over the fish of the sea, and over the fowl of the air, and over the cattle, and over all the earth, and over every creeping thing that creepeth upon the earth.*
>
> *So **God created man** in his own image, in the image of God created he him; male and female created he them.*
>
> > *Genesis 1:26-27, emphasis added*

> *And the **Lord God formed man** of the dust of the ground, and breathed into his*

106

nostrils the breath of life; and man became a living soul.
And the Lord God planted a garden east-ward in Eden; and there he put the man whom he had formed.

Genesis 2:7-8, emphasis added

In Genesis 1, it is **God that created man**; however, in Genesis 2 the **Lord God formed man**.

After conducting a detailed comparison, is there really a difference between Genesis 1 and Genesis 2?

Why would ***God*** be credited with doing everything in Genesis 1 but the ***Lord God*** is stated as doing everything in Genesis 2?

Consider this perspective. My name is Nycole but, depending on my relationship with certain individuals, I can be called Nycole, Mommy, Honey, Nikki or Rosebud.

We have learned that the word "God" is translated as *Elohim*. Elohim is the general name for God as the Creator. It reflects God as the all-powerful, awesome and majestic Creator who is responsible for creating all things. Genesis 2 did not reference God, instead it stated the *Lord God*. The name *Lord God* means Yahweh.

Yahweh is God's personal name and is used to indicate God having a relationship with man. If Yahweh is noted in Genesis 2 as executing all the work and Elohim is noted in Genesis 1 as doing all the creating, then the difference must be directly related to the making of man. If you look closely at Genesis 1 and Genesis 2, you will notice that the mention of Lord God began when the *forming* of man was discussed.

In Genesis 1, Elohim *created* man as a spirit. However, according to Genesis 2, Yahweh *formed* man. He formed the shape of a human being on earth. What I am telling you is that Elohim created all the things in Genesis 1, including man which He *created* as a spirit in the spiritual realm. Yet it is Yahweh that *forms* man and shapes man in the dust. It is Yahweh that is personally involved with forming the earthly being for man and afterward, He breathed His breath of life into the shaped dust of man. It is Yahweh that brings forth this human to be alive on the earth. Therefore, it was not Elohim the Creator that formed man - it was Yahweh that formed man.

Genesis 1 is God creating everything related to heaven and earth realms, in totality.

Genesis 2 is a more detailed view of what happened as it relates specifically to man, in the earthly realm.

Everything from Genesis 2:4 to the end of the chapter are the details surrounding Yahweh's purposeful approach to the relationship with man in the earthly realm.

At first glance, Genesis 1 and Genesis 2 appear to cover the same creative activities, but we have revealed that the information is not identical. Is this due to a different name or a slightly different terminology? No, it contrasts because the Lord God, Yahweh, is the personal, covenant God involved with forming man, causing man to come alive, providing for man, caring for man, and having relationship with man, but also due to the fact that Genesis 2 reveals the activities surrounding the forming of man occurred in a different location than where Elohim is stated as creating in Genesis 1.

PLACEMENT

And the Lord God formed man of the dust
of the ground, and breathed into his nostrils
the breath of life; and man became a living
soul.
  And the Lord God planted a garden east-
ward in Eden; and there he put the man
whom he had formed.

Genesis 2:7-8

The aforementioned scripture indicates that the Lord God (Yahweh) puts man in a garden, which was not a small piece of ground used to grow vegetables, fruit, herbs and flowers. This garden was a paradise.

Man was not created or formed in the Garden. Man was created and formed in the world. Yahweh made a garden, specifically for Adam, in a place called Eden, where they could have relationship. A place in the world but not of or like the world. Yahweh also put in vegetation, which according to Genesis 2:9 was a different kind of food specifically for Adam to enjoy in the Garden, distinct from the provision in the world. Thus, man is taken out of the world that Elohim created and placed by Yahweh in a smaller area, a paradise, facing eastward, toward the rising of the sun. How wonderful that man's point of view in the place designed specifically for him is facing the sunrise!

Yahweh engages and communicates with man in the Garden and it is at that point that the male being is called Adam. It is important to understand that man is called Adam only *after* he is formed and *after* his interaction with Yahweh. Adam had been given everything he needed to survive and thrive. He was still in the image and after the likeness of "Us" and still maintained his dominion and ability to replenish and subdue the earth. Additionally, Yahweh communed, interacted and visited with Adam in the Garden, not in the world, but in the place Yahweh specifically created for him. This is relationship!

Yahweh then decided it was not good for Adam to be in paradise by himself and determined that Adam needed a "help meet", so Yahweh formed animals - but not like Elohim (God) had created animals. Elohim (God) made beasts of the earth *from the waters.* Yahweh (Lord God) made specific beasts in the Garden, namely beasts of the field and fowl of the air, formed *out of the dust of the ground*, specifically for Adam, yet there was not found a help meet among the animals that was suitable for Adam. Therefore, Yahweh made a woman as a help meet for Adam and brought her to him in the Garden of Eden.

Yahweh has made everything for this man. What he needed, what was suitable for him, and fully equipping him with function and position to rule and reign in the place that Yahweh, the relational God, had set up for him. Yahweh had prepared the Garden of Eden within the world yet separate, specifically for those with whom He'd have relationship. There, in the place that Yahweh determined as best, is where Yahweh talked with Adam, spent time with him, taught him, interacted with him and brought animals to him and watched him name them. Yes, Yahweh relates and gives man instruction, direction and communication as well as the ability to hear and understand His voice. Yahweh walked with both Adam and the woman in the cool of the day. Not in the world, but in the place that Yahweh had prepared especially for them. This place was made with a spiritual relationship in mind.

Man is the purposeful creation of the One True God, and represents something special and unlike all the other creatures that God has created. Man is uniquely created in the image and after the likeness of God, formed with relationship in mind by Yahweh, vested with authority over the world and everything in the world and commanded to reproduce. He is placed in a beautiful paradise, interacting with a relational God, facing the sunshine and stocked with everything he could ever need, then given a wife - all to maintain the order and pattern that God has set. God was pleased and said that it was very good! Everything else God created He said was good. But, once man was formed and placed in his rightful place, it was so good that, after this, God rested!

God has done the same thing for you. He desires a relationship. He wants to put you in a place where you can commune with Him and interact with Him, where you have everything you need outside of the world.

The Bible states that evening and morning were the 6th day. We see with the creation and formation of man that God is bringing things from chaos to order.

Let's review what God accomplished in the first six days of The Creation including the 6th setting of order:

~~Day 1~~ - 1st setting of order:
Establishing what is good (moral activity) based on what God determines - setting the pattern of good/moral versus immoral.

~~Day 2~~ - 2nd setting of order:
Setting the pattern of the earthly realm in the midst of the spiritual realm.

~~Day 3~~ - 3rd setting of order:
Setting the pattern of reproduction for the earth realm.

~~Day 4~~ - 4th setting of order:
Setting the pattern of time for the earth realm.

~~Day 5~~ - 5th setting of order:
Setting the pattern of souls and life of water and flying animals as well as the introduction of blessings to reproduce.

~~Day 6~~ - 6th setting of order:
Setting the pattern of the human kind that has relationship with God and operates as the human manifestation of God in the earthly realm.

Over the past several chapters, we have been discussing The Creation and what took place in "The Beginning". In dissecting the 1st and 2nd book of Genesis, Holy Spirit has revealed some very eye opening things that have helped us comprehend what took place in the beginning that was different from what we thought.

During the previous chapters I disclosed:

- How God made the distinction between morality versus immorality by bringing forth light.

- The Creation is depicting how God is taking things from chaos to order.

- That God is setting a pattern for order. Order according to His way of doing things.

While progressing through the succession of what God created, I came across something that peaked my interest at the point in The Creation where God commissioned someone referred to as "Us" to make man, and it was noted that there was no direct mention in the details of The Creation that indicated who God was speaking to nor coordinated with, to make this man. Being a curious person, I wanted to know who "Us" was in the context of the text and who was involved in assisting God in making man. God made and created everything else by Himself. Why now, does He commission others to make man with Him? If man was made in the image and after the likeness of "Us", then perhaps we could ascertain who "Us" is by understanding the components of this man that was proposed during his creation.

Additionally, a side of God has been revealed in the creation of man, that has allowed us to see God in a new way.

WHO WAS PRESENT?

Now that the composition of man is understood, let's tackle who the ones that God refers to as "Us" are and how they made man.

I think the best way to address this question is to begin by reviewing what has already been disclosed. Based on the previous chapters discussing Genesis 1 and Genesis 2, it has been revealed who was present in the beginning, during The Creation as well as the components of man. Hopefully, this information will provide assistance in understanding who "Us" is.

I would like to begin with who was there in the beginning, during The Creation. According to Genesis 1:1-2, God, the spirit of God, and darkness were present, but the first thing God did was to impact darkness.

Genesis 1:3-4 states that God brings forth light. This reveals the possibilities of who those referred to as "Us" could be:

> **God** (Genesis 1:1)
> **Spirit of God** (Genesis 1:2)
> **Darkness** (Genesis 1:2)
> **Light** (Genesis 1:4)

Knowing that God was breaking the influence of darkness, that tells us that God did not approve of darkness, and if God wanted it separate from the light and light was good, then I can deduce that He would not include darkness in the creation of man. Therefore, darkness can be disregarded as a potential collaborator. That leaves the following to be present before man was created:

> **God** (Genesis 1:1)
> **Spirit of God** (Genesis 1:2)
> ~~Darkness (Genesis 1:2)~~
> **Light** (Genesis 1:4)

In Genesis 2:7, it was also identified that the Lord God (Yahweh) was involved directly with the making of man. Therefore, the list of those present now could include:

> **God/Elohim/The Creator** (Genesis 1:1)
> **Spirit of God** (Genesis 1:2)
> **Light** (Genesis 1:4)
> **The Lord God/Yahweh** (Genesis 2)

Genesis 1 and Genesis 2 have indeed provided insight

into who was present when man was created and formed; however, there are additional scriptures in the Bible that can also contribute to the endeavor of identifying who is the "Us" that God collaborated with during the creation of man. I think Proverbs 8 gives a clue. Due to the length of Proverbs 8, I am only documenting the applicable verses.

> *Doth not wisdom cry? and understanding put forth her voice?*
>
> *The Lord possessed me in the beginning of his way, before his works of old.*
>
> *I was set up from everlasting, from the beginning, or ever the earth was.*
>
> *When there were no depths, I was brought forth; when there were no fountains abounding with water.*
>
> *Before the mountains were settled, before the hills was I brought forth:*
>
> *While as yet he had not made the earth, nor the fields, nor the highest part of the dust of the world.*
>
> *When he prepared the heavens, I was there: when he set a compass upon the face of the depth:*
>
> *When he established the clouds above: when he strengthened the fountains of the deep:*
>
> *When he gave to the sea his decree, that the*

119

*waters should not pass his commandment:
when he appointed the foundations of the
earth:*

*Then I was by him, as one brought up with
him: and I was daily his delight, rejoicing
always before him;*

*Rejoicing in the habitable part of his earth;
and my delights were with the sons of men.*
                                      Proverbs 8:1, 22-31

This passage of scripture surely reveals that someone was present in the beginning, even when man was created and formed. This means that the list of participants in the creation and formation of man now includes Wisdom and Understanding. Let's look at what we have so far.

God/Elohim/The Creator (Genesis 1:1)
Spirit of God (Genesis 1:2)
Light (Genesis 1:4)
The Lord God/Yahweh (Genesis 2)
Wisdom and Understanding (Proverbs 8)

Another passage of scripture comes to mind.

*In the beginning was the Word, and the
Word was with God, and the Word was God.*

The same was in the beginning with God.

*All things were made by him; and without
him was not any thing made that was made.*

In him was life; and the life was the light of

men.

*And the light shineth in darkness; and the
darkness comprehended it not.*

John 1:1-5

That increases the collaborators present in the beginning
to include:

God/Elohim/The Creator (Genesis 1:1)
Spirit of God (Genesis 1:2)
Light (Genesis 1:4)
The Lord God/Yahweh (Genesis 2)
Wisdom and Understanding (Proverbs 8)
The Word (John 1:1)

Before progressing forward, something in John 1 verse
5 needs our attention. Do you recall Genesis 1:3, when the
very first thing that God brought forth was light, even before
creating the heaven and the earth? Do you also recall the
differentiation of light in the beginning as opposed to lights
in the 4th setting of order? Remember, the light that God
spoke on day 1 was to be placed in the world in the midst of
the waters and was to rule *in* the world to set order of moral
versus immoral activity, according to the righteousness of
God which was among, but separate from, the darkness. Alternatively, the lights (sun, moon, planets, and stars) were
to rule in the firmament of heaven and provide a light source
for and upon the earth.

The light that God brought forth in Genesis 1:3, was the
*light **of** men*, not *lights **for** men*. According to John 1:4-5,
that *light* and The Word are one and the same as it is the

121

light of men!

Therefore, our final list includes the following as those being present and having input in the creation of man:

God/Elohim/The Creator (Genesis 1:1)
Spirit of God (Genesis 1:2)
Light/The Word (Genesis 1:4 & John 1:1)
The Lord God/Yahweh (Genesis 2)
Wisdom and Understanding (Proverbs 8)

THE TRINITY

Like many of you, I was always taught that the Trinity, (known as The Father, The Son, and The Spirit of God) is who created mankind, but no one ever explained how Wisdom was present in the beginning and whether the Father was also there, as part of the Trinity. So, I prayed and asked Holy Spirit if the Trinity was there in the beginning and to show me in scripture that the Father was there. In the wee hours of a Saturday morning, He spoke.

THE FATHER

The first thing the Holy Spirit revealed to me were the attributes and functions of a Father:

- Provider
- Protector
- Gives Direction/Teacher
- Gives Identity
- Disciplinarian
- Participates in bringing forth life

Then He said to consider what the Lord God (Yahweh) did and what He gave when He formed man. I ascertained that the Lord God (Yahweh) encompassed all of the attributes stated above.

Let's check it out:

Provider - According to Genesis 2:8, the Lord God placed man in the Garden of Eden, providing him a nice home as well as an abundance of food.

Protector - The Lord God (Yahweh) provided protection by warning Adam of the outcome of eating of the Tree of the Knowledge of Good and Evil. Yahweh also made man a protector by giving him the ability to be God's representative on the earth and by giving him dominion over the animals by protecting the order and pattern that He had set.

Direction/Teacher - The Lord God (Yahweh) instructed Adam and watched as he named the animals and showed His approval with Adam's aptitude.

Identity - After the Lord God (Yahweh) had interaction with man, He called him Adam. He gave man a name and an identity.

Disciplinarian - The Lord God disciplined Adam and the woman when they disobeyed. (I refer to her as *the woman* because she was not named Eve until after they disobeyed.)

Participates in bringing forth life - It was also revealed that it was the Lord God (Yahweh) that brought forth man into the earth by forming a shape from the dust and gave it His own breath. When His breath hit the shape, the shape became a living human being.

The Bible reveals that the Lord God encapsulates the attributes of a Father as scripture reveals that He is a provider, disciplinarian, protector, teacher, gives identity, and participates in bringing forth life - all of which are done by a good father to his son. In the event that my rationale is a bit of a stretch for you, consider this.

Holy Spirit said to me, "In order to have a son, you must have a father." Would you agree? I would like to point your attention to the Book of Luke.

The third chapter of Luke recounts the baptism of Jesus by John the Baptist. After Jesus is baptized, the Bible states the genealogy of Jesus. This lineage begins with Jesus and lists all ancestors up to, and including Adam. The account of

Luke is as follows:

> *Now when all the people were baptized, it came to pass, that Jesus also being baptized, and praying, the heaven was opened,*
>
> *And the Holy Ghost descended in a bodily shape like a dove upon him, and a voice came from heaven, which said, Thou art my beloved Son; in thee I am well pleased.*
>
> *And Jesus himself began to be about thirty years of age, being (as was supposed) the son of Joseph, which was the son of Heli,*
>
> *Which was the son of Matthat, which was the son of Levi, which was the son of Melchi, which was the son of Janna, which was the son of Joseph,*
>
> *Which was the son of Mattathias, which was the son of Amos, which was the son of Naum, which was the son of Esli, which was the son of Nagge,*
>
> *Which was the son of Maath, which was the son of Mattathias, which was the son of Semei, which was the son of Joseph, which was the son of Juda,*
>
> *Which was the son of Joanna, which was the son of Rhesa, which was the son of Zorobabel, which was the son of Salathiel, which was the son of Neri,*

Which was the son of Melchi, which was the son of Addi, which was the son of Cosam, which was the son of Elmodam, which was the son of Er,

Which was the son of Jose, which was the son of Eliezer, which was the son of Jorim, which was the son of Matthat, which was the son of Levi,

Which was the son of Simeon, which was the son of Juda, which was the son of Joseph, which was the son of Jonan, which was the son of Eliakim,

Which was the son of Melea, which was the son of Menan, which was the son of Mattatha, which was the son of Nathan, which was the son of David,

Which was the son of Jesse, which was the son of Obed, which was the son of Booz, which was the son of Salmon, which was the son of Naasson,

Which was the son of Aminadab, which was the son of Aram, which was the son of Esrom, which was the son of Phares, which was the son of Juda,

Which was the son of Jacob, which was the son of Isaac, which was the son of Abraham, which was the son of Thara, which was the son of Nachor,

127

Which was the son of Saruch, which was the son of Ragau, which was the son of Phalec, which was the son of Heber, which was the son of Sala,

Which was the son of Cainan, which was the son of Arphaxad, which was the son of Sem, which was the son of Noe, which was the son of Lamech,

Which was the son of Mathusala, which was the son of Enoch, which was the son of Jared, which was the son of Maleleel, which was the son of Cainan,

Which was the son of Enos, which was the son of Seth, which was the son of Adam, which was the son of God.

Luke 3:21-38

In verse 38, scripture plainly states according to the lineage of Jesus, that *Adam was the son of God.* That makes God a Father!

The aforementioned scriptures in Luke 3, coupled with the understanding of how the Lord God (Yahweh) interacted with Adam, confirms that the Father was also present in the beginning.

Those that were on the scene having input in the beginning, were the same that God was speaking to when proposing the making of mankind and they were all also involved with making the heavenly and earthly realms.

Herein is proof that the Trinity: the Father, the Word, and the Spirit of God, plus Wisdom were all present in the beginning. This is the "Us" that God was referring to when making man.

For those of you who are saying, "Wait, Wisdom isn't part of the Trinity." You are absolutely correct. Wisdom is not part of the Trinity. The Bible says the Lord (Yahweh) *possessed* wisdom, so wisdom was possessed by the Lord God, not independent of Him.

We now see for ourselves that this "Us" that had been commissioned to make man is God the Father, God the Word, and God the Spirit. Now I know you noticed that I didn't say "the Trinity is the Father, Son, and Holy Spirit". Instead, I said the Father, *the Word* and the Holy Spirit. Let me explain.

> Before Jesus came to earth, the Trinity was the Father, ***the Word*** and the Spirit; however, it is only ***after*** Jesus came to earth, the Trinity is the Father, ***the Son*** and the Spirit.

Let me show you.

If we were to continue to read a little further in John 1, we would obtain more understanding.

> *And the Word was made flesh, and dwelt among us, (and we beheld his glory, the glory as of the only begotten (only-born) of the*

129

Father,) full of grace and truth.

John 1:14

Scripture reveals that sometime later (*after* The Creation), the Word becomes flesh and recall, we recently discussed how Genesis 1 and John 1 revealed that the Word and light are one and the same - brought forth to be the light of the world. John 8:12 further proves this to be true.

> *Then spake Jesus again unto them, saying, I am the light of the world: he that followeth me shall not walk in darkness, but shall have the light of life.*

John 8:12

The Word becomes Jesus in the earthly realm sent to be the human manifestation of God on the earth, and we know Jesus is the Son of God. So, *before* Jesus makes His appearance on the earth, the Trinity is the Father, *the Word* and the Spirit of God. *After* Jesus comes to earth, the Trinity consists of the Father, *the Son (Jesus)*, and the Spirit of God.

Therefore, the reference to "Us" is indeed the Trinity of God - those that are responsible for making man and giving them the representation and position of Them on the earth.

~~DAY 7~~ - 7TH SETTING OF ORDER

Thus the heavens and the earth were finished, and all the host of them.

And on the seventh day God ended his work which he had made; and he rested on the seventh day from all his work which he had made.

And God blessed the seventh day, and sanctified it: because that in it he had rested from all his work which God created and made.

Genesis 2:1-3

REST

The word *rested* often means "to come to an end or stop".

The 7th succession of order reveals that God has completed all His activities for The Creation. He has also made this 7th day special by setting the order for it to be a day of resting. But did you notice that scripture did not indicate that evening and morning was the 7th day? Every day since beginning creation, God stated that evening and morning were a day; however, when He has completed His work, there is no indication of evening and morning. Why?

Look back on what was disclosed about evening and morning in chapter 4. You learned that evening and morning were not indicative of time, and were more so about God taking things from chaos to order. Genesis 1:31 states that

God saw *everything* that He had made and that it was "very good", which meant it was pleasing and moral according to God's way of doing things.

That being the case, God didn't indicate that evening and morning were the 7th day because God, with wisdom, instituted *everything* to bring order. With the culmination of man in position, morality had been set on the earth.

God ended His work and rested because He had fulfilled all things needed to bring order to the earth and left His representative on the earth with the responsibility to rule and reign over all that He had made. Man was to maintain that order and continue in the pattern with the function and position that God fattened and filled him with. Therefore, God could end His work because He had positioned someone else, who was equipped, to be left in charge.

Man was the final setting of order, the final pattern needed on the earth for the will and purpose of God. The dominion of the mysterious secret power that controlled and inhabited the abode of the dead was broken and life was initiated with God's representative being in place. Thus God has finished His work!

In thinking back over the past chapters about what occurred in the beginning, you should now understand the order that God has set. A brief overview is presented on the following page.

Setting of Order in Succession

1ˢᵗ day - 1ˢᵗ setting of order:

> Determining what is good (moral activity) based on what God determines - setting the pattern of good/moral vs. immoral.

2ⁿᵈ day - 2ⁿᵈ setting of order:

> Setting the pattern of the earthly realm in the midst of the spiritual realm.

3ʳᵈ day - 3ʳᵈ setting of order:

> Setting the pattern of provision for the natural realm.

4ᵗʰ day - 4ᵗʰ setting of order:

> Setting the pattern of time and set times dedicated to God for the natural realm.

5ᵗʰ day - 5ᵗʰ setting of order:

> Setting the pattern of souls, life, and reproduction of life with His blessing for the natural realm.

6ᵗʰ day - 6ᵗʰ setting of order:

> The final work of God - setting the pattern of land animals and man as well as setting the pattern of man's relationship with God, separated from the world, ruling and reigning in the earth as a representative of God.

7ᵗʰ day - 7ᵗʰ setting of order:

> Setting the pattern of rest.

THE BLUEPRINT

Remember when we started this book, I told you that
the book of Genesis teaches about the beginning
and we would focus on how that was the beginning
of God revealing Himself and His immeasurable love.

You've seen God set the pattern of order. He began setting the pattern since He brought forth light.

> The real pattern and order that God set was
> a pattern of His love through relationship
> and salvation.

Here's what I mean.

The Creation is the blueprint. When God rested on day
7, He left His earthly representative on the earth to main-

tain His order. From that point on, God gave man power and authority to maintain order as His representative on the earth and put the devil under foot. This was the final 'chaos to order' with relationship restored and salvation claimed through Jesus Christ. How?

According to Genesis 3, Adam and the woman disobeyed the Lord God, which took them out of His presence and broke their relationship with the Father that wanted a relationship with them. But, before the heavenly and earthly realms were created, God brought forth light and we learned that the light and the Word are one and the same. We also learned that the Light and the Word are Jesus and we know that Jesus died for our sins so that we could be brought back into relationship with the Father through salvation.

Just like Adam, you were created in the world, but God desires to take you out of the world and put you in a place designed by Him, specifically for you, where He provides, sustains, and cares for you. Where He gives you everything you need in provision, protection, direction, discipline, identity, life and deity to maintain His pattern of order in the earthly realm. He gives you dominion and shows you how to use it. He teaches you. It's His paradise made with you in mind. It's a place of peace, joy, unity, and His presence. A place created just for you, where He meets with you, engages and interacts with you. A place free from the reign of darkness, chaos, terror, dread, and torment. A place where it's you and Him. I am not only referring to eternal life in heaven, I am also referring to your time on this earth. God is your Father. He loves you and wants you to live your best life in His presence on earth and forever in His presence when you leave this earth. This is His pattern - this is the order that He has set.

Man was intended to be in relationship with the Lord God and interact with Him in peace with everything he needs. Man was also designed to be His representative in the earthly realm.

Although the sin of Adam affected our relationship with the Lord God, God ensured, before anything was created, that we would have a choice to be in relationship with Him through salvation.

Therefore, The Creation is the beginning of salvation and the beginning of relationship. Salvation started in the beginning with the bringing forth of light. Before man was made, created or formed, God's love for you started in the beginning. He set this pattern prior to you making your entrance on the earth, ensuring that you would be given the chance to again be in relationship with Him as His child and He would be your Father. God loves you and He still desires a deeper relationship with you.

So let me ask you a question. Are you in the world amidst chaos, darkness, gloom, torment and fear? Or are you in order, a place of peace, love, joy, with salvation and relationship with God through Christ?

As much revelation and understanding of scripture that you have received through this book, you need to ask yourself, *"Why is it important to me? Why did God feel the need to tell me all of this?"* The answer is simple. It is because

God loves you and He made you like Him, created to maintain the set order of Him in the earth. If you are a son or daughter of the Lord God, the next question that needs to be addressed is, *"Are you maintaining order on the earth or are you a conduit of chaos, disorder, confusion, darkness, terror and gloom on the earth? Are you maintaining order according to God's set pattern, according to His righteousness or are you being led by the world and your human nature?"* Your purpose, as a believer, is to maintain God's order, but so many believers are in full blown chaos, confusion, disorder, and living according to the ways of the world. That is not God's ultimate desire for you.

The order that God set didn't begin with Adam and end with Jesus! Like Adam, God desires you to come out of the world and into His way of doing things. You were created to be a representative of God on the earth. You were formed to be in relationship with God. You were given responsibility. You were given dominion. Many of us are living so far below what God has determined for us because we are out of order.

What God started in the beginning is still His desire for you now. That desire is for you to see the distinction between light and darkness, between chaos and order. You have to choose which one will have headship over you. Like Adam and the woman, you have been given a choice to choose God as your Lord and Master, and to choose order, or to choose darkness, which is chaos. Your choice determines who has rulership over you and will determine if you live a life, now and for eternity, in chaos or in order. The choice is yours.

And that's what really happened in the beginning!

It is my prayer that this book has helped you to see God and His love for you through the events of The Creation in a way that you have never seen before. My hope is that you have come to understand how much God loves you, your importance to God and how much He desires to have a continuous relationship with you. He had you on His mind before the beginning of time and He has you on His mind now!

God desires to engage with you, to show you His love to a greater degree. He wants to reveal to you why He created and formed you. You are part of His master plan and exquisite pattern. He has a purpose for you and within that purpose, He wants to show you what real life is, not determined by the world system, but according to His love. God did not make a mistake when He made you. He strategically created and formed you so beautifully in His image and after His likeness. He also provided a way for you to have a relationship with Him now and in eternity through Jesus Christ. His foresight is immeasurable. His love is everlasting. His joy is incomprehensible. His desire for a relationship with you is unending. His arms are always open for you!

God longs for you to be out of chaos and in a place of order. I pray that the eyes of your understanding have been enlightened and you begin to discover the intentional love that God has for you. A love like you've never known. A love He has had for you since the beginning!

NOTES

Introduction

1. Strong, J., Kohlenberger, J. R., & Swanson, J. A. The strongest Strong's exhaustive concordance of the Bible (J. R. Kohlenberger & J. A. Swanson, Eds.). Grand Rapids, Mich.: Zondervan. 2001

Day 1

2. Strong, J., Kohlenberger, J. R., & Swanson, J. A. The strongest Strong's exhaustive concordance of the Bible (J. R. Kohlenberger & J. A. Swanson, Eds.). Grand Rapids, Mich.: Zondervan. 2001

3. Strong, J., Kohlenberger, J. R., & Swanson, J. A. The strongest Strong's exhaustive concordance of the Bible (J. R. Kohlenberger & J. A. Swanson, Eds.). Grand Rapids, Mich.: Zondervan. 2001

4. Strong, J., Kohlenberger, J. R., & Swanson, J. A. The

strongest Strong's exhaustive concordance of the Bible (J. R. Kohlenberger & J. A. Swanson, Eds.). Grand Rapids, Mich.: Zondervan. 2001

5. Lexico.com [Internet]. Oxford: Oxford University Press; 2021 [cited 2021 Aug 08]. Available from: https://www.lexico.com/definition/darkness

6. Strong, J., Kohlenberger, J. R., & Swanson, J. A. The strongest Strong's exhaustive concordance of the Bible (J. R. Kohlenberger & J. A. Swanson, Eds.). Grand Rapids, Mich.: Zondervan. 2001

7. Strong, J., Kohlenberger, J. R., & Swanson, J. A. The strongest Strong's exhaustive concordance of the Bible (J. R. Kohlenberger & J. A. Swanson, Eds.). Grand Rapids, Mich.: Zondervan. 2001

Day 2

8. Strong, J., Kohlenberger, J. R., & Swanson, J. A. The strongest Strong's exhaustive concordance of the Bible (J. R. Kohlenberger & J. A. Swanson, Eds.). Grand Rapids, Mich.: Zondervan. 2001

Day 3

9. Strong, J., Kohlenberger, J. R., & Swanson, J. A. The strongest Strong's exhaustive concordance of the Bible (J. R. Kohlenberger & J. A. Swanson, Eds.). Grand Rapids, Mich.: Zondervan. 2001

10. Strong, J., Kohlenberger, J. R., & Swanson, J. A. The strongest Strong's exhaustive concordance of the Bi-

ble (J. R. Kohlenberger & J. A. Swanson, Eds.). Grand
Rapids, Mich.: Zondervan. 2001

11. Strong, J., Kohlenberger, J. R., & Swanson, J. A. The
strongest Strong's exhaustive concordance of the Bible (J. R. Kohlenberger & J. A. Swanson, Eds.). Grand
Rapids, Mich.: Zondervan. 2001

12. Strong, J., Kohlenberger, J. R., & Swanson, J. A. The
strongest Strong's exhaustive concordance of the Bible (J. R. Kohlenberger & J. A. Swanson, Eds.). Grand
Rapids, Mich.: Zondervan. 2001

13. Strong, J., Kohlenberger, J. R., & Swanson, J. A. The
strongest Strong's exhaustive concordance of the Bible (J. R. Kohlenberger & J. A. Swanson, Eds.). Grand
Rapids, Mich.: Zondervan. 2001

14. Strong, J., Kohlenberger, J. R., & Swanson, J. A. The
strongest Strong's exhaustive concordance of the Bible (J. R. Kohlenberger & J. A. Swanson, Eds.). Grand
Rapids, Mich.: Zondervan. 2001

15. Strong, J., Kohlenberger, J. R., & Swanson, J. A. The
strongest Strong's exhaustive concordance of the Bible (J. R. Kohlenberger & J. A. Swanson, Eds.). Grand
Rapids, Mich.: Zondervan. 2001

16. Strong, J., Kohlenberger, J. R., & Swanson, J. A. The
strongest Strong's exhaustive concordance of the Bible (J. R. Kohlenberger & J. A. Swanson, Eds.). Grand
Rapids, Mich.: Zondervan. 2001

17. Strong, J., Kohlenberger, J. R., & Swanson, J. A. The

strongest Strong's exhaustive concordance of the Bible (J. R. Kohlenberger & J. A. Swanson, Eds.). Grand Rapids, Mich.: Zondervan. 2001

Day 4

18. Strong, J., Kohlenberger, J. R., & Swanson, J. A. The strongest Strong's exhaustive concordance of the Bible (J. R. Kohlenberger & J. A. Swanson, Eds.). Grand Rapids, Mich.: Zondervan. 2001

19. Strong, J., Kohlenberger, J. R., & Swanson, J. A. The strongest Strong's exhaustive concordance of the Bible (J. R. Kohlenberger & J. A. Swanson, Eds.). Grand Rapids, Mich.: Zondervan. 2001

20. Strong, J., Kohlenberger, J. R., & Swanson, J. A. The strongest Strong's exhaustive concordance of the Bible (J. R. Kohlenberger & J. A. Swanson, Eds.). Grand Rapids, Mich.: Zondervan. 2001

21. Lexico.com [Internet]. Oxford: Oxford University Press; 2021 [cited 2021 Aug 08]. Available from: https://www.lexico.com/definition/illicit

22. Lexico.com [Internet]. Oxford: Oxford University Press; 2021 [cited 2021 Aug 08]. Available from: https://www.lexico.com/definition/illegal

23. Lexico.com [Internet]. Oxford: Oxford University Press; 2021 [cited 2021 Aug 08]. Available from: https://www.lexico.com/definition/immoral

24. Strong, J., Kohlenberger, J. R., & Swanson, J. A. The strongest Strong's exhaustive concordance of the Bi-

ble (J. R. Kohlenberger & J. A. Swanson, Eds.). Grand
Rapids, Mich.: Zondervan. 2001

25. Lexico.com [Internet]. Oxford: Oxford University Press; 2021 [cited 2021 Aug 08]. Available from: https://www.lexico.com/definition/chaos

26. Lexico.com [Internet]. Oxford: Oxford University Press; 2021 [cited 2021 Aug 08]. Available from: https://www.lexico.com/definition/disorder

27. Lexico.com [Internet]. Oxford: Oxford University Press; 2021 [cited 2021 Aug 08]. Available from: https://www.lexico.com/definition/order

28. Wikipedia contributors. In Wikipedia, The Free Encyclopedia [Internet]; [updated 2022 Jan 20; cited 2022 Jan 31]. Available from: https://en.wikipedia.org/w/index.php?title=Pattern&oldid=1066853101

29. Strong, J., Kohlenberger, J. R., & Swanson, J. A. The strongest Strong's exhaustive concordance of the Bible (J. R. Kohlenberger & J. A. Swanson, Eds.). Grand Rapids, Mich.: Zondervan. 2001

30. Strong, J., Kohlenberger, J. R., & Swanson, J. A. The strongest Strong's exhaustive concordance of the Bible (J. R. Kohlenberger & J. A. Swanson, Eds.). Grand Rapids, Mich.: Zondervan. 2001

31. Strong, J., Kohlenberger, J. R., & Swanson, J. A. The strongest Strong's exhaustive concordance of the Bible (J. R. Kohlenberger & J. A. Swanson, Eds.). Grand Rapids, Mich.: Zondervan. 2001

Day 5

32. Strong, J., Kohlenberger, J. R., & Swanson, J. A. The strongest Strong's exhaustive concordance of the Bible (J. R. Kohlenberger & J. A. Swanson, Eds.). Grand Rapids, Mich.: Zondervan. 2001

33. Strong, J., Kohlenberger, J. R., & Swanson, J. A. The strongest Strong's exhaustive concordance of the Bible (J. R. Kohlenberger & J. A. Swanson, Eds.). Grand Rapids, Mich.: Zondervan. 2001

34. BlueLetterBible.org [Internet]. Strong's Hebrew Lexicon (kjv): Blue Letter Bible; 2021 [cited 2021 Aug 08]. Available from: https://www.blueletterbible. org/lexicon/h8577/kjv/wlc/0-1/

35. BlueLetterBible.org [Internet]. Strong's Hebrew Lexicon (kjv): Blue Letter Bible; 2021 [cited 2021 Aug 08]. Available from: https://www.blueletterbible. org/lexicon/h8565/kjv/wlc/0-1/

36. Strong, J., Kohlenberger, J. R., & Swanson, J. A. The strongest Strong's exhaustive concordance of the Bible (J. R. Kohlenberger & J. A. Swanson, Eds.). Grand Rapids, Mich.: Zondervan. 2001

37. Strong, J., Kohlenberger, J. R., & Swanson, J. A. The strongest Strong's exhaustive concordance of the Bible (J. R. Kohlenberger & J. A. Swanson, Eds.). Grand Rapids, Mich.: Zondervan. 2001

38. Strong, J., Kohlenberger, J. R., & Swanson, J. A. The strongest Strong's exhaustive concordance of the Bi-

ble (J. R. Kohlenberger & J. A. Swanson, Eds.). Grand Rapids, Mich.: Zondervan. 2001

Day 6

39. Strong, J., Kohlenberger, J. R., & Swanson, J. A. The strongest Strong's exhaustive concordance of the Bible (J. R. Kohlenberger & J. A. Swanson, Eds.). Grand Rapids, Mich.: Zondervan. 2001

40. Strong, J., Kohlenberger, J. R., & Swanson, J. A. The strongest Strong's exhaustive concordance of the Bible (J. R. Kohlenberger & J. A. Swanson, Eds.). Grand Rapids, Mich.: Zondervan. 2001

41. Strong, J., Kohlenberger, J. R., & Swanson, J. A. The strongest Strong's exhaustive concordance of the Bible (J. R. Kohlenberger & J. A. Swanson, Eds.). Grand Rapids, Mich.: Zondervan. 2001

42. Strong, J., Kohlenberger, J. R., & Swanson, J. A. The strongest Strong's exhaustive concordance of the Bible (J. R. Kohlenberger & J. A. Swanson, Eds.). Grand Rapids, Mich.: Zondervan. 2001

43. Lexico.com [Internet]. Oxford: Oxford University Press; 2021 [cited 2021 Aug 08]. Available from: https://www.lexico.com/definition/representation

44. Strong, J., Kohlenberger, J. R., & Swanson, J. A. The strongest Strong's exhaustive concordance of the Bible (J. R. Kohlenberger & J. A. Swanson, Eds.). Grand Rapids, Mich.: Zondervan. 2001

45. Lexico.com [Internet]. Oxford: Oxford University Press; 2021 [cited 2021 Aug 08]. Available from: https://www.lexico.com/definition/distinction

46. Strong, J., Kohlenberger, J. R., & Swanson, J. A. The strongest Strong's exhaustive concordance of the Bible (J. R. Kohlenberger & J. A. Swanson, Eds.). Grand Rapids, Mich.: Zondervan. 2001

47. Strong, J., Kohlenberger, J. R., & Swanson, J. A. The strongest Strong's exhaustive concordance of the Bible (J. R. Kohlenberger & J. A. Swanson, Eds.). Grand Rapids, Mich.: Zondervan. 2001

48. Strong, J., Kohlenberger, J. R., & Swanson, J. A. The strongest Strong's exhaustive concordance of the Bible (J. R. Kohlenberger & J. A. Swanson, Eds.). Grand Rapids, Mich.: Zondervan. 2001

49. Strong, J., Kohlenberger, J. R., & Swanson, J. A. The strongest Strong's exhaustive concordance of the Bible (J. R. Kohlenberger & J. A. Swanson, Eds.). Grand Rapids, Mich.: Zondervan. 2001

50. Strong, J., Kohlenberger, J. R., & Swanson, J. A. The strongest Strong's exhaustive concordance of the Bible (J. R. Kohlenberger & J. A. Swanson, Eds.). Grand Rapids, Mich.: Zondervan. 2001

For information on bookings or to place an
order:

Nycole Donelson Ministries
40 Burton Hills Blvd.
Suite 200
Nashville, TN 37215

www.nycoledonelson.com

CPSIA information can be obtained
at www.ICGtesting.com
Printed in the USA
LVHW010754160322
713507LV00015B/1695